A "Noble Bet" in Early Care and Education

Lessons from One Community's Experience

Brian P. Gill

Jacob W. Dembosky

Jonathan P. Caulkins

Prepared for the
Heinz Endowments

RAND Education

RAND

The research described in this report was supported by the Heinz Endowments.

Library of Congress Cataloging-in-Publication Data

Gill, Brian P., 1968–
    A "nobel bet" in early care and education : lessons from one community's experience / Brian P. Gill, Jake Dembosky, Jonathan P. Caulkins.
        p. cm.
    "MR-1544."
    Includes bibliographical references.
    ISBN 0-8330-3162-7
    1. Child care services—Pennsylvania—Allegheny County—Case studies. 2. Education, Preschool—Pennsylvania—Allegheny County—Case studies. 3. Children with social disabilities—Services for—Pennsylvania—Allegheny County—Case studies. I. Dembosky, Jake. II. Caulkins, Jonathan P. (Jonathan Paul), 1965– III.Title.

HQ778.67 .A5 G55 2002
362.7'09748'85—dc21

                                                                2002021366

RAND is a nonprofit institution that helps improve policy and decisionmaking through research and analysis. RAND® is a registered trademark. RAND's publications do not necessarily reflect the opinions or policies of its research sponsors.

Published 2002 by RAND
1700 Main Street, P.O. Box 2138, Santa Monica, CA 90407-2138
1200 South Hayes Street, Arlington, VA 22202-5050
201 North Craig Street, Suite 102, Pittsburgh, PA 15213
RAND URL: http://www.rand.org/
To order RAND documents or to obtain additional information, contact Distribution Services: Telephone: (310) 451-7002;
Fax: (310) 451-6915; Email: order@rand.org

RAND was commissioned by the Heinz Endowments to evaluate the vision, organization, administration, and operation of the Early Childhood Initiative (ECI), a major effort to improve early care and education (ECE) for low-income children from birth through age five in Pittsburgh, Pennsylvania, and the surrounding communities of Allegheny County. ECI was conceived and designed from 1994 to 1996, and operated under the auspices of the United Way (UW) of Allegheny County from 1996 through 2000. Its quality of service and child welfare outcomes are being examined separately by a research team from the University of Pittsburgh and Children's Hospital in Pittsburgh; that team's findings to date are reported in Bagnato, 2002.

RAND's research effort involved, first and foremost, approximately one hundred intensive, confidential interviews with a diverse group of stakeholders: United Way managers, ECI staff, members of the foundation community and other funders, neighborhood representatives, early childhood service providers, business leaders involved in ECI, government officials, academic experts, and early childhood advocates. RAND also obtained and examined a substantial amount of written documentation pertaining to ECI, primarily through the assistance of ECI management and neighborhood agencies. These documents were used not only to understand ECI's history, but also to examine its enrollment and costs. Finally, the RAND study team explored existing empirical literature on ECE.

Although ECI led to the establishment of new, high-quality ECE services in several communities, it failed to achieve many of its major goals, despite the good intentions of everyone involved and despite the support of a wide array of community leaders. This report relays the results of RAND's evaluation, which sought both to explain why ECI was not more successful and to suggest how future initiatives might produce better results. It describes ECI's goals and objectives and articulates the breadth of the initiative's ambition to create a comprehensive new system for delivering ECE to low-income children in Allegheny County. It also presents a narrative history of ECI—from its genesis in 1994–1996 through its scale-down and departure from the United Way at the end of 2000—and a critical analysis of ECI's business plan and operations, explicating a number of reasons that the initiative fell short of its goals. Finally, since the report aims to be more than a postmortem analysis, it offers lessons for the future, alternative models for ECE initiatives, and public-policy implications. This report should have relevance not only for ECI's stakeholders in Allegheny County, but also for funders, program developers, and policymakers around the country who are working on large-scale initiatives related to a variety of social service reforms.

CONTENTS

FIGURES

TABLES

BACKGROUND AND REPORT'S OBJECTIVES

The Early Childhood Initiative (ECI) of Allegheny County (including the city of Pittsburgh), Pennsylvania, was an ambitious effort to provide high-quality early care and education (ECE) services to at-risk children. Launched in 1996 under the auspices of the United Way (UW) of Allegheny County, ECI aimed within five years to serve 7,600 at-risk children ages zero (birth) to five in 80 low-income neighborhoods, at an average cost of $4,000 to $5,000 per child and a total cost of $59 million over the five-year period. By intervening early in the lives of at-risk children with high-quality services, ECI hoped to improve their preparation for kindergarten, promote their long-term educational attainment, and give them the early tools to help them become productive, successful members of society.

While the long-term benefits of high-quality ECE had been suggested by a number of small-scale, demonstration programs, ECI aimed to be the first in the nation to establish a comprehensive system for delivering high-quality ECE services on a countywide scale. Moreover, ECI intended to provide services through programs that were chosen and operated at the community level by local neighborhood agencies. Finally, ECI aimed to become financially sustainable over the long term, when the initial infusion of dollars from foundations and private donors was exhausted. It planned a lobbying effort to persuade the state of Pennsylvania to commit to fund the initiative at the end of the five-year startup period.

Midway through the fourth year of implementation (2000), when it was clear that the state lobbying effort had failed, that ECI was far short of its enrollment targets, and that cost per child was significantly higher than expected, ECI planners decided to scale down the initiative and convert it to a demonstration program. In April 2001, the program—renamed as the ECI Demonstration Program—was transferred from UW to the Office of Child Development at the University of Pittsburgh, where it was placed under new management.

RAND's evaluation, commissioned by the Heinz Endowments (ECI's largest funder) after ECI had been sharply scaled back, was motivated by the desire to understand why ECI fell short of its objectives and to learn from its mistakes. This report summarizes ECI's organizational history, analyzes and explains critical weaknesses that hindered ECI's ability to succeed, and articulates lessons to inform the design and implementation of future large-scale reform initiatives, whether in ECE or in other areas of social services. Our findings are based, first of all, on intensive interviews with nearly one hundred stakeholders, including UW managers, ECI staff, funders, neighborhood representatives, early childhood service providers, business leaders involved in ECI, government officials, academic experts, and early childhood advocates. We also obtained and examined ECI's documentary records (including business plans, enrollment records, and financial records), constructed quantitative models to analyze cost and enrollment data, and explored existing empirical literature on ECE.

AMBITIOUS AIMS AND MAJOR OBSTACLES

ECI's goals were ambitious. It aimed (1) to provide high-*quality* ECE services, (2) to do so on a large *scale* (to serve 7,600 children in 80 neighborhoods within five years at a cost of $4,000 to $5,000 per child), (3) to use a *community*-driven approach, and (4) to achieve *sustainability* through a commitment of state funding. Adding significantly to the challenge were major political, institutional, economic, and cultural obstacles. These included pervasive low quality among many of the existing child-care providers, political ambivalence about the appropriate public role in ECE, possible underappreciation of the benefits of quality (by policymakers and parents alike), wide variations in physical and organizational resources in low-income neighborhoods, and the challenges of building a large, new initiative from scratch. One early supporter of ECI in the business community described it publicly as a "noble bet."[1] In our view, that description is quite appropriate. ECI's goals were noble, but their achievement would be difficult and required a calculated gamble. Indeed, to have achieved all of ECI's aims would have been a heroic feat.

The implication is this: *Given the scope of the aims and the scope of the obstacles, success required that ECI have a clear sense of market realities in early care and education, a well-designed theory of action, an effective strategy for inducing a commitment of public funding, and a coherent organizational structure.* This report explains how weaknesses in each of these areas undermined ECI's success in terms of its scale, community, and sustainability goals, if not its quality goals.

THE BOTTOM LINE

Although evidence from a separate evaluation suggests that ECI may have succeeded in promoting high-quality ECE programs, it was far less successful in achieving its other goals.

Quality

Quality of service and child welfare outcomes, which were not part of RAND's charge, are being examined separately by the SPECS (Scaling Progress in Early Childhood Settings) team from the University of Pittsburgh and Children's Hospital in Pittsburgh. RAND did not review the SPECS methods, so we simply note the findings to date of the SPECS team here. According to the SPECS report (Bagnato, 2002), ECI succeeded in promoting quality in participating ECE programs and favorable outcomes for participating children. More specifically, the report states that ECI children demonstrated effective social and behavioral skills and that they went on to succeed in kindergarten and first grade, as measured by low rates of grade retention and referral to special education. The findings reported by

---

[1]The term was coined by Charles J. Queenan, Jr., a prominent Pittsburgh attorney.

the SPECS team are substantially what ECI's planners aimed to achieve for participating children.

Scale

At its peak (around May 2000), ECI served only about 680 children, which is one-quarter of the number expected to be served at that point in time and less than one-tenth of the total number targeted for service.

While ECI served fewer children than intended, its hours of service per child were higher than intended because, contrary to the plan's assumption that most children would be in part-day services, virtually all children were in full-day services. Even accounting for this difference, however, ECI at its peak was providing only about half as many child-hours of service as the original business plan had intended for that point in time.

Even if ECI had been able to scale up more quickly, it could not have served 7,600 children, because costs per child were substantially higher than expected. In 1999 (year three of implementation), ECI's cost averaged $13,612 per child-year.[2] Although this is not dramatically different from the cost of some other, widely cited high-quality ECE interventions,[3] it is three times as high as the cost expected in the original business plan ($4,407 in year three). As we discuss in depth throughout this report, the business plan made a number of mistakes that contributed to the underestimation of costs. Here we mention three reasons that were prominent. First, ECI provided far more hours of service per child than the plan anticipated, because virtually all children were served in full-day programs. Second, the plan assumed that operational cost per child was the same at all levels of enrollment, failing to recognize that cost per child is inevitably substantially higher for providers that are less than 100 percent enrolled. Third, ECI's plan required a substantial bureaucratic struc-

---

[2]1999 was the last full year of ECI's full-scale operation (as well as the last year for which we were able to obtain financial data). Details on the methodology and assumptions for calculating costs are provided in the Appendix.

[3]For example, the High/Scope Perry Preschool Project cost an estimated $12,148 per child (in 1996 dollars) (Karoly et al., 1998).

ture both centrally and at the neighborhood level, and it was unduly optimistic about the administrative costs associated with this structure.

Community

ECI's community-driven approach had some successes and a number of failures. Devolution of authority to the neighborhood level succeeded in a few neighborhoods where local leaders eagerly joined the ECI process and established plans that led to a strong working relationship with ECI management (ECIM) and, ultimately, the creation of new, high-quality ECE programs operated by neighborhood-based agencies. Moreover, community leaders in a number of neighborhoods affected by ECI joined together to establish an ongoing support and advocacy network for early childhood and school readiness issues.

But disappointment is widespread in many of the neighborhoods that were targeted by ECI. Some local leaders felt that ECI did not live up to its promise of permitting neighborhoods to define their needs and the ECE services they wanted. In their view, ECI's process for approving neighborhood plans imposed unreasonable delays, and ECI imposed a narrow definition of quality that precluded local discretion. This left substantial resentment in some neighborhoods, especially those that did not get an early start in the process and were eventually cut off when ECI was scaled down in 2000. Even in neighborhoods that successfully launched ECE programs under ECI's sponsorship, lead agencies felt undermined by constantly changing program rules and requirements.

Sustainability

Although ECI helped to raise the profile of ECE as an important policy issue in communities around Pennsylvania and in state government, it failed in its explicit goal of achieving a state commitment to support the initiative with public funds. An effort to change the initiative to make better use of existing state funding streams was only partly successful, and it led to a power struggle over the direction of ECI, as well as to frustration and resentment in the neighborhoods. The sustainability of the two remaining neighborhood agencies supported by ECI has not yet been demonstrated and will be a major goal for these agencies over the next three years while their foundation funding continues.

Positive Aspects of ECI's Legacy

ECI's failure to achieve its greatest ambitions should not obscure the positive aspects of its legacy. ECI helped to build the capacity of a number of low-income neighborhoods to provide ECE services that are apparently of high quality. It succeeded in helping several Head Start providers become licensed to provide full-day services. It increased public awareness of the importance of quality in Pittsburgh and around the state and reportedly motivated quality improvements in some major nonparticipating child-care centers in Allegheny County. And it demonstrated the ability of the Pittsburgh community to mobilize large-scale support and funding from diverse constituencies and people with differing political perspectives. Finally, ECI's troubles serve to illuminate the serious public-policy dilemmas associated with ECE.

We now turn to the major task of the report: explaining the mistakes that undermined ECI's success with respect to its scale, community, and sustainability goals.

A COMPLICATED THEORY OF ACTION AND ADMINISTRATIVE STRUCTURE

At the time of ECI's inception, no models existed of high-quality ECE delivered on a large scale through grassroots, neighborhood control. ECI therefore needed to develop its own "theory of action" to explain how the initiative would work. According to the theory of action developed by the original planners (depicted in Figure S.1), ECI was to have a central administration (housed within UW) that would fund, supervise, and monitor (with stringent quality standards) lead agencies in each community. Each lead agency would in turn fund and supervise the participating ECE providers, which would serve children and their families. In addition, the central administration (ECI management, or ECIM) was to provide technical assistance to lead agencies, which would in turn provide such assistance to ECE providers.

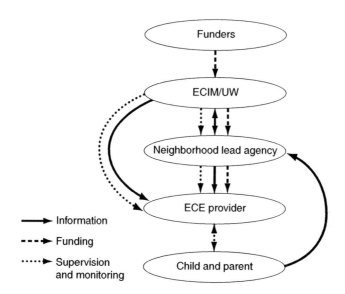

Figure S.1—ECI's Theory of Action

This theory of action proved to be cumbersome and problematic. While most of ECI's theory of action concerned the central administration and neighborhood agencies, the ultimate goals of high-quality ECE services for large numbers of children around the county were to be served by the relationship between providers and families. ECI's theory of action created an extensive structure above that relationship rather than addressing it more directly. This put several layers of organization between the funders and the primary intended beneficiaries (i.e., the children to be served) and led to a number of implementation problems.

Administrative Costs

One consequence of ECI's multilayered theory of action was that each layer of administration added to the initiative's cost. The original business plan projected that the cost of ECI's central administration at UW would amount to $286 per child (or 6.5 percent of a total cost of $4,407 per child) in year three of implementation. In fact, central administrative costs in year three (1999) were $1,231 per child (or 9 percent of the total cost of $13,612). The theory of action simultaneously imposed substantial top-down requirements and created additional structures in each neighborhood, making high administrative costs inevitable.

The Challenges of Community Control

At the same time it established a hierarchical bureaucracy, ECI's theory of action aimed to permit neighborhoods to direct participating local programs. Devolution of authority to the community level requires a tradeoff: Neighborhood-led programs may be more robust and effective than those imposed from the outside, but implementation is not likely to proceed quickly. ECI's planners failed to appreciate how much time neighborhood groups would need to mobilize, assess residents' needs, identify space for child-care centers, develop detailed proposals, and establish programs.

ECI's business plan did not acknowledge the extent to which quality control and community control might be in tension. ECI's insistence on its own definition of quality inevitably placed constraints on the degree of freedom to be exercised by communities. When ECI was launched, neighborhoods were told to "dream big"; some were disappointed when they found that their dreams were not always consistent with the vision of ECIM. Although neighborhood agencies endorsed the principle of high-quality service provision, some chafed under a quality monitoring process that they perceived as excessively rigid.

A Flawed Administrative Structure

Compounding these problems was a complicated administrative structure for ECI's leadership. ECI lacked an independent board with the authority to resolve conflicts and make key decisions. ECIM staff were nominally UW employees, but they were never comfortably integrated into the larger UW organization. ECIM reported to several different UW managers at different points in time, often lacking a clear chain of command. A proliferation of volunteer oversight committees further confused administration and diffused authority. And when key staff departed, individuals who had been hired to serve a specific role were given responsibilities outside their primary experience and expertise.

ECI's complex leadership structure had several negative consequences. First, the community planning process was slow, because plans had to be reviewed by several layers of committees. Second, the response to changing conditions related to the increased demand for full-day services was slow. Third, confusion over who had the authority to make key operational and strategic decisions permitted disagreements between ECIM and UW management to escalate into full-blown, unresolved power struggles.

ECIM and UW management prioritized the goals of the initiative differently. For ECIM, maintaining high quality was the paramount goal. UW management worried about serving substantial numbers of children and achieving sustainability. When costs per child turned out to be much higher than expected, ECI's goals came into tension with each other, putting ECIM and UW management at loggerheads. The weakness of the organizational structure delayed the conflict's resolution. Communication with funders and business leaders broke down because UW management and ECIM disagreed over what they should be telling these stakeholders. At the community level, lead agencies and providers received mixed signals about ECI rules and procedures. As a result, support for ECI declined among funders and business leaders, and confidence in the initiative suffered in the neighborhoods.

LACK OF ATTENTION TO DEMAND, SUPPLY, AND INCENTIVES

ECI's original business plan made assumptions about the population of children that would be served, the mix of services (e.g., full-day versus half-day, center versus family child-care) that would be provided, and the participation of existing ECE providers. Many of these assumptions turned out to be far off the mark, largely because the planners paid insufficient attention to demand, supply, and incentives. A number of ECI's problems that were related to enrollment and costs might have been avoided if the business plan had better anticipated how parents, ECE providers, and neighborhood agencies would respond to ECI.

The Demand for Full-Day, Center-Based Services

The business plan failed to anticipate that parents and neighborhood agencies might gravitate toward the highest-cost option among the services ECI offered, which ranged from part-day, Head Start–like enrichment and literacy programs to full-day, center-based care and education. The plan assumed that 71 percent of children would be served in low-cost, part-day programs. In fact, virtually all children were served in full-day programs, most in new centers. Hence, one major reason that ECI cost more per child than expected was that ECI provided more intensive services (on average) than expected.

ECI underestimated the demand for full-time programs in part because it underestimated the proportion of eligible children whose mothers were in the workforce. Welfare reform—passed in Pennsylvania in the summer of 1996—was relevant in bringing women into the workforce, but low-income mothers had already been joining the labor force in growing numbers prior to welfare reform. Moreover, a parental preference for full-day care is unsurprising if parents are given a choice of full- or part-day care and both options are largely or entirely subsidized. Large numbers of parents—whether low- or high-income, employed or not—are likely to prefer more hours of child care and education if they are offered at little or no additional cost. This is essentially the choice that ECI offered. The incentives for neighborhood agencies were similar: Told by ECI to "dream big," most sought to establish new child-care centers.

The Cost of Relying on New Providers

Although the business plan expected that many existing providers would be used, in practice many were left out. This occurred for three reasons. First, ECIM believed that many existing providers operated at so low a level of quality that they were incapable of providing high-quality services. Second, some community planning groups chose to exclude existing providers. Third, some existing providers chose not to participate, either because they considered the quality standards and monitoring process too intrusive or because they were informal, unregistered providers not wishing to become part of the formal child-care system. ECI's greater-than-expected reliance on new providers meant that it could not reach as many children as hoped and resulted in higher capital costs as well.

Extensive reliance on new centers also meant that ECI had to endure the high costs of the startup period, during which center staff have to be employed but enrollment is relatively low. More generally, ECI's original business plan mistakenly assumed that centers that were less than fully enrolled could serve children for the same cost per child as fully enrolled centers could (i.e., it assumed that operating costs at a center were fully variable). Such an assumption might have been reasonable for pre-existing centers, for which ECI intended to provide a capitated reimbursement amount for each child served. In fact, however, the great majority of ECI children were served in newly established centers. Line item funding was provided for new centers, which needed to hire staff prior to enrolling their first children. This meant that in practice the centers' operating costs were largely fixed, regardless of the number of children served.

When ECI centers opened, enrollments grew gradually over time and in most cases never reached 100 percent of capacity. In 1999, average enrollment in ECI centers was 72.6 percent of capacity (increasing over the course of the year). As a result, operating cost per child was higher than projected in the original business plan. The fault here lies not with the lead agencies or the providers, but with the variable-cost assumption of the original business plan, which was not realistic.

EXPLAINING ECI'S COSTS

The total cost per child in 1999 ($13,612) was 3.1 times as high as the expected cost ($4,407). The planners underestimated all components of cost: operating, capital, and administrative. Using simulations to correct some of the mistaken assumptions of the original business plan, we were able to estimate the magnitude of different drivers of ECI's cost overruns. Figure S.2 depicts ECI's original cost projections, its actual costs, and the results of two simulations.

The second bar in the figure shows the results of adjusting the original cost projections using the actual service mix provided by ECI in 1999. The shift to full-day, center-based services dramatically in-

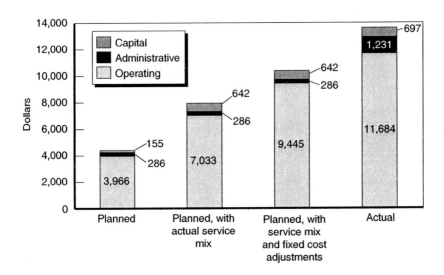

Figure S.2—Effect of Service Mix and Fixed Costs on Cost per Child-Year, 1999

creased both operating and capital costs. If the business plan had anticipated the actual service mix, its estimate of the expected cost per child would have risen from $4,407 to $7,961.

The third bar accounts not only for the actual service mix, but also for the fixed costs of operating new child-care centers. The simulation in this case was based on incomplete data, so the results should be interpreted cautiously. Because a portion of operating costs may be variable, the estimate represents an upper bound. Nevertheless, it makes clear that the ECI business plan substantially underestimated costs because it did not recognize that operating costs in new centers would be largely fixed. If the business plan had accounted for fixed costs and anticipated the actual service mix, its estimate of the expected cost per child would have risen to as much as $10,373.

In total, the two flawed assumptions explain as much as 65 percent of the difference between the planned and actual cost per child (again, this is an upper-bound estimate). Figure S.3 shows how central administrative costs and additional operating and capital costs (not already explained by the service mix) compare to the flawed business plan assumptions in explaining the total difference between

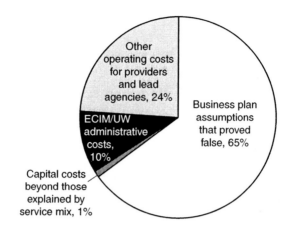

**Figure S.3—Factors Explaining the Difference Between
Planned and Actual Cost per Child-Year, 1999**

planned and expected cost per child. Higher-than-expected central administrative costs account for 10 percent of the difference. Capital costs beyond those attributable to the service mix explain less than 1 percent of the difference. After accounting for underestimates related to service mix, fixed operating costs, capital costs, and central administrative costs of ECIM and UW, the remaining neighborhood-level costs for lead agencies and service provision explain 24 percent of the difference between expected and actual cost per child (which may be a slight underestimate if the fixed cost adjustment is overestimated).

The interpretation of ECI's total cost of $13,612 per child depends to a great extent on the frame of reference. Compared to the budgeted amount of $4,407, it seems astonishingly high. But it is important to remember that high-quality, full-day ECE programs generally cost substantially more than $4,407. Nevertheless, it is clear that ECI's business plan and operation ensured that costs would be dramatically higher than expected. The theory of action virtually guaranteed that administrative costs would be high. In addition, planners failed to anticipate the predictable demands of parents and lead agencies, which moved the initiative toward providing the more-expensive, full-time, center-based care. Indeed, ECI ultimately looked quite different from what many of its original advocates and funders had intended.

THE FAILURE TO SECURE STATE SUPPORT

ECI's plan to secure state funding ultimately failed because of existing obstacles and the particular strategy pursued. The obstacles were many. First, the benefits of high-quality ECE programs are diffuse, whereas the costs are concentrated. A strong societal benefit/cost ratio may not be sufficient to persuade the state to foot the bill when many of the benefits will not accrue to the state's treasury. Second, most of the benefits of high-quality ECE programs accrue over the long term (e.g., program participants not getting involved in crime as teenagers and adults), whereas the costs are borne up front. Third, the amount of funding that planners hoped the state would contribute to ECI—most of the $26 million annual cost when it reached countywide scale—was large enough that it would inevitably raise issues of regional fairness among Pennsylvania political leaders.

Finally, voters and policymakers were and still are ambivalent about public funding of ECE. Some voters and policymakers feel strongly that child care is a private responsibility of parents rather than a public responsibility of the state. The views of leadership at the state level clearly make a difference, and, despite growing support for public funding of ECE in many states, Pennsylvania's state government has a history of conservatism when it comes to funding ECE programs.

Independent of these obstacles, ECI's strategy for obtaining state funding was misguided. First, although ECI planners made some attempts to engage state officials, they did not ensure that state policymakers had a full, substantive, and early role in the initiative's design.

Second, and more fundamentally, ECI came into conflict with the goals and operation of Pennsylvania's existing system of child-care subsidies for low-income families. The shift in the ECI service mix to full-day programs switched its public identification from an education initiative to a child-care initiative and increased its financial dependence on the existing state system of child-care subsidies. ECI's initial conflict with the state subsidy system stemmed from its failure to acknowledge the state's preference for parental choice in child care. ECI also came into conflict with the state's desire, via welfare reform, to induce parents on public assistance to enter the workforce. ECI's primary goal was to provide high-quality early education to low-income children—regardless of whether their parents were working. The primary goal of the state child-care subsidy system, by contrast, is to provide incentives and means for parents receiving public assistance to move into the workforce. Even if ECI's planners disagreed with the state's priorities, it was important to recognize that a direct conflict with those priorities would seriously undermine the likelihood of state support for ECI.

This conflict became a serious operational problem for ECI as it became increasingly dependent on the state's existing subsidy system. UW sought to reduce costs and make ECI more compatible with the state subsidy system, but its efforts created major internal conflicts and undermined ECI's support in the neighborhoods. Moreover, these efforts did not ultimately reduce costs enough to make ECI sustainable using existing or foreseeable levels of state subsidies.

LESSONS FOR THE FUTURE

ECI's weaknesses suggest a number of lessons for future large-scale reform initiatives:

- Planners should focus on clear goals and well-defined services. In ECI's case, its quality, scale, and community-control goals often came into conflict with each other, especially when different stakeholders prioritized the goals differently or defined quality differently.

- An ambitious, large-scale initiative should have an independent board and a clear administrative structure that promotes strong leadership.

- A clean, direct theory of action more effectively promotes an initiative's goals.

- Careful consideration of demand, supply, and responses to incentives is essential to anticipating unintended consequences.

- Planners should make every effort to include all relevant stake-holders early in the planning process.

- Critical, independent review is essential from the start. Review should be conducted by someone who can identify flaws without fear of retribution, is not a member of the original advocacy group, has appropriate substantive expertise, and will invest time and energy in the review commensurate with the project's importance.

- Large-scale initiatives benefit from a substantial investment in planning and often are well served by initial piloting on a smaller scale.

- Bold visions require hardheaded plans that acknowledge political and policy realities.

ALTERNATIVE MODELS FOR ECE REFORM

We gathered information on four promising ECE initiatives currently operating in Pennsylvania and elsewhere. The Chicago Child-Parent Center program operates through the Chicago public schools, offering high-quality preschool to low-income children. In southeastern Pennsylvania, Child Care Matters is a UW-operated initiative that works to improve the quality of existing ECE providers by providing them with technical assistance and resources as well as a "quality supplement" incentive if they become accredited with the National Association for the Education of Young Children (NAEYC). Focus on Our Future, in York, Pennsylvania, likewise provides resources to promote accreditation; it also funds professional development for ECE workers. In Chicago, Focus on Quality has helped over 100 centers become accredited with NAEYC, while a public awareness campaign has promoted parental awareness of the value of high-quality ECE. Formal evaluation results are as yet available for only one of these programs (the Chicago Child-Parent Centers), but we believe that each program represents a promising approach that funders, policymakers, and ECE practitioners may wish to consider. These programs by no means constitute the full array of promising ECE initiatives. Nevertheless, each suggests an alternative approach to scaling up high-quality ECE services. In contrast to ECI, each has a narrower focus on a more limited number of goals. None places much emphasis on the goal of community control, and most focus on existing providers, thereby making the scale-up process more straightforward and usually faster.

Future large-scale ECE initiatives might consider any of these possibilities, or might instead consider a parent-centered approach. For example, planners might choose to distribute funds as quality-focused supplements to the existing state subsidy system. Parents would be permitted to use "quality vouchers" at any provider that met a designated quality standard. If an existing standard, such as NAEYC accreditation, is considered insufficient, a separate quality monitoring system could be established to identify high-quality providers and enforce standards. Additional grants might be available to providers seeking to improve their quality in order to become eligible for the "quality vouchers."

We do not mean to suggest that pursuing a community-driven approach is necessarily bad. But funders, program planners, and policymakers need to understand that community-driven processes inevitably take time. Moreover, communities may have desires and interests that differ from those of the planners; in consequence, an approach that takes the community's desires seriously must be prepared to accept results that may differ from those the planners and funders originally intended. An approach that simultaneously aims to permit community control and to impose top-down bureaucratic control may well lead to disappointment on all sides.

Although we found no examples among the initiatives described above, there may be models that would both take the community's desires more seriously and provide more appropriate incentives, permitting communities to "dream big" while controlling costs and ensuring quality. In addition, it is worth pointing out that parent-centered models are implicitly community based because they are driven by the desires of parents in the community.

IMPLICATIONS FOR PUBLIC POLICY

As ECI's planners recognized, inducing large and sustained changes in the ECE universe requires public action. State and federal policymakers can exercise substantial influence over conditions in the ECE market, if they choose to do so. The ECI experience raises several broad public-policy issues that may provide guidance for policymakers.

The first such issue concerns the demand for quality. Evidence suggests that parents do not have a high demand for high-quality ECE services, at least as understood by ECE experts (Blau, 2001). But parental knowledge and preferences are not set in stone. Policymakers (and local planners) may be able to increase the demand for high-quality services through public awareness campaigns and parent education efforts.

Policymakers may also wish to directly address quality in child care. One increasingly popular approach to raising the quality of ECE services is a tiered subsidy system. Under such a system, each provider receives a per-child subsidy based on the provider's level of quality. Providers then have an incentive to improve their quality. States have the discretion to use federal welfare funds to raise subsidy amounts for higher-quality providers; many have already done so. In addition, greater public investment in the education and training of ECE workers might serve as a useful complement to a tiered subsidy system.

ECI illuminates the tension that exists between two purposes: serving needy children and providing incentives for parents to work. In most states (including Pennsylvania), the primary purpose of child-care subsidy systems for low-income parents is to encourage them to move off welfare and into the labor force. A substantial number of low-income children are ineligible for subsidies because their parents do not meet the requirements of welfare-reform laws. In consequence, any ECE policy that is tied to welfare laws will fail to reach many at-risk children. Policymakers who wish to promote the availability of high-quality ECE services for all disadvantaged children need to take a different approach.

Many policymakers and voters resist the idea of separating child-care subsidies from employment requirements. They often see employment requirements not only as a way to provide appropriate incentives to welfare mothers, but also as a way to distinguish between "deserving" and "undeserving" poor in the distribution of government benefits. Whether this latter purpose is appropriate is a matter of basic values, such as fairness and justice, and is not easily susceptible to empirical policy analysis. But policymakers may wish to consider the costs to society of a child-care policy that focuses on the deservingness of parents rather than the welfare of children.

ACKNOWLEDGMENTS

This report benefited greatly from assistance from many individuals. First of all, we thank our colleagues Jim Hosek, Becky Kilburn, and Tom Glennan, who advised us on the investigation and analysis at various points. We learned much from their extensive experience and wisdom. Shelley Wiseman helped us improve the organization and writing. Our reviewers, Megan Beckett and Michal Perlman, read the entire draft with care and provided valuable feedback that substantially improved the final report. Jeri O'Donnell and Janet DeLand expertly edited and formatted the report in record time.

We thank Marge Petruska and Maxwell King of the Heinz Endowments for funding the study and giving us the opportunity to carry it out. Mardi Isler deserves special thanks. She was extraordinarily helpful throughout the course of the study in providing a substantial amount of archival material from ECI's records, and she was unfailingly professional in responding to our repeated inquiries. And we thank Charles J. Queenan, Jr., for the phrase "noble bet" that is used in our title.

Our greatest debt is owed to the dozens of individuals who generously gave their time to talk to us about their experiences and insights with respect to the Early Childhood Initiative. These included ECI staff, United Way managers, neighborhood agency representatives, government officials, business leaders, foundation staff, and early childhood service providers. Because we promised respondents that they would remain anonymous, we cannot name them individually here. Without their assistance, however, this study could not have been undertaken.

GLOSSARY

ACF	Administration for Children and Families
AFDC	Aid to Families with Dependent Children
CAP	Chicago Accreditation Partnership
CCDF	Child Care and Development Fund
CCIS	Child Care Information Service
CCM	Child Care Matters
CDA	Child Development Associate
CEO	Chief executive officer
CMAEYC	Chicago Metropolitan Association for the Education of Young Children
CPC	Chicago Child-Parent Center
DPW	Department of Public Welfare (Pennsylvania)
ECE	Early care and education
ECI	Early Childhood Initiative
ECIDP	ECI Demonstration Program
ECIM	Early Childhood Initiative Management
FCC	Family child care

FOF	Focus on Our Future
FOQ	Focus on Quality
HUD	U.S. Department of Housing and Urban Development
Lead agency	The community-based agency selected by each neighborhood to supervise ECI services
NAEYC	National Association for the Education of Young Children
NAFCC	National Association for Family Child Care
NICHD	National Institute of Child Health and Development
OCD	Office of Child Development (at the University of Pittsburgh)
PRC	Preliminary review committee
RFNP	Request for Neighborhood Plans
SPECS	The Scaling Progress in Early Childhood Settings group, a research team from the University of Pittsburgh and Children's Hospital in Pittsburgh
TANF	Temporary Assistance for Needy Families
T.E.A.C.H.	Teacher Education and Compensation Helps
UW	United Way
UWSEPA	United Way of Southeastern Pennsylvania

Chapter One

INTRODUCTION

THE GOALS OF THE EARLY CHILDHOOD INITIATIVE

The Early Childhood Initiative (ECI) of Allegheny County (including the city of Pittsburgh), Pennsylvania, was an ambitious, large-scale effort to provide high-quality early care and education (ECE) services to disadvantaged infants, toddlers, and preschool-age children. As understood by ECI's planners, such services go well beyond the simple supervision of children while parents work or attend school. Following the lead of the National Association for the Education of Young Children (NAEYC), the leading professional organization in the field, ECI's initiators believed that high-quality ECE has a strong educational component, with a focus on developmentally appropriate care, play, and learning activities, regardless of whether it is provided in preschool programs (including Head Start programs), child-care centers, or family child-care homes, and regardless of whether it is provided on a part-day or full-day basis.

ECI was launched in 1996 under the auspices of the United Way (UW) of Allegheny County. Its goal was to provide, within five years, high-quality ECE services to 7,600 children ages zero (birth) to five in 80 of the county's low-income neighborhoods at a total expected cost of $59.4 million over the five-year period. By intervening early in the lives of at-risk children with intensive high-quality care and education, ECI hoped to significantly improve these children's chances of being prepared for kindergarten, excelling in school, graduating, and becoming productive, successful members of society. To focus on at-risk children, ECI's planners targeted neighborhoods that had high rates of poverty, welfare receipt, and unemployment, as well as large proportions of both students dropping out of high school and female-headed families.[1] While the long-term benefits of high-quality ECE had been demonstrated by a number of small-scale, demonstration programs over the years, ECI aimed to create a model for the nation by being the first to establish a comprehensive system for delivering high-quality ECE services on a countywide scale.

Moreover, ECI intended to provide high-quality ECE services on a large scale through programs that were chosen and supervised at the community level by local neighborhood agencies, consistent with a growing emphasis on community direction among social service planners across the nation (see, e.g., Center for the Study of Social Policy, 1996; Schorr, 1997; and Zigler, Kagan, and Hall, 1996). Each targeted neighborhood was expected to select a local "lead agency" to supervise ECI's activity in the neighborhood. ECI sought to give community residents and organizations considerable discretion over the kinds of high-quality services that would be offered in each neighborhood (e.g., existing versus new child-care providers, center-based programs versus family child-care homes) and over the administration and delivery of new programs. Each neighborhood was intended to have ownership of its particular ECI programs.

Finally, ECI aimed to make its high-quality ECE programs financially sustainable over the long term—i.e., when the initial, five-year infusion of dollars from foundations and private donors was exhausted. ECI's planners recognized that, to achieve sustainability, a major commitment of public funding would be necessary. The business plan therefore called for an effort over the first three years of ECI's operation to persuade the state of Pennsylvania to commit to taking over primary responsibility for funding the initiative at the end of the five-year startup period. Planners expected that if ECI could be

---

[1]In 1994, a study conducted by the University of Pittsburgh's Office of Child Development identified over 18,000 children under age six in Allegheny County who were living in poverty (Farber, Williams, and Groark, 1994). Many of these children were concentrated in specific neighborhoods. A significant number had been born to teenage mothers, were low-birthweight babies, or had received late prenatal care. A large body of research suggests that such children are, over the course of their lives, at high risk of dropping out of school or of becoming pregnant as teenagers, addicted to drugs or alcohol, involved in crime, or dependent on public assistance.

demonstrated as an effective model for providing high-quality ECE services, state policymakers could be persuaded to ensure funding for the long term—and possibly to adopt ECI as a model for the rest of the state. Their optimism was fueled by a national policy context in which many states were beginning to pay increasing attention to and invest increasing resources in ECE.

ECI's planners hoped that ECI would "raise the bar" for all ECE providers, motivating them to improve quality. They also hoped that ECI would help bring order to a fragmented ECE system. For example, ECI administrators wanted to pool funding from various sources, such as state child-care subsidy programs, subsidies for children in the child-protection system, and federal subsidies to child-care providers (along with ECI funds), to more effectively provide ECE services to at-risk children.

For the first five years of implementation, ECI was to depend primarily on private funds raised locally from various foundations, corporations, and individuals, with smaller amounts of funding from parent fees and government sources. ECI's original business plan, approved by the UW at the initiative's launch in 1996, estimated that the total cost would be $59.4 million over five years.[2] Although philanthropic contributions would constitute the bulk ($51 million) of the startup cost, the plan recognized that buy-in from the state was essential for ECI's long-term sustainability, and it therefore included a scale-down contingency in case the state could not be persuaded to assume responsibility. If state officials had not made a commitment by the end of the third year of implementation to take over funding after the five-year startup period, ECI was to be phased out. New children would no longer be enrolled in ECI programs, and those already being served would be allowed to continue only until the end of year five (2001). If state officials did make the commitment, implementation would continue, with the expectation that about 7,600 children would be receiving ECI services at the end of five years.

---

[2]Planners projected that $51 million (86 percent) could be raised through local philanthropic sources; $6 million (10 percent) from government sources, including direct grants, state child-care subsidies, and other government programs; and $1.8 million (3 percent) from parent fees (with the remainder from accrued interest).

THE AIMS AND METHODS OF THIS STUDY

ECI ultimately failed to achieve many of its goals. Our evaluation, commissioned by the Heinz Endowments (ECI's largest funder) after ECI had been sharply scaled back, was motivated by the desire to understand why ECI fell short of its objectives and to learn from its mistakes. This report seeks to summarize ECI's organizational history, to analyze and explain critical weaknesses that hindered ECI's ability to succeed, and to articulate lessons that will inform the design and implementation of future large-scale, public-private initiatives, whether in the field of ECE or in other areas of social services. We believe the report will be useful to several different audiences. First, we think it may help ECI's stakeholders more fully understand some of the key sources of the initiative's difficulties. Second, the lessons it sets forth about the design and implementation of large-scale, public-private initiatives are aimed at community leaders and funders not only in western Pennsylvania but around the country. Finally, we hope the report illuminates some of the large public-policy dilemmas that should be of interest to policymakers examining ECE issues everywhere.

The first major research task informing our findings was a series of intensive interviews over the course of 2001 with nearly one hundred stakeholders who were asked questions about their involvement with ECI, their perceptions of ECI's goals and vision, and their knowledge of ECI's operations. Rather than choosing a limited sample of stakeholders, we tried to approach comprehensiveness in selecting interviewees. This meant that we sought to interview virtually everyone involved in decisionmaking about ECI, from conception to business plan, implementation, neighborhood activities, state government interaction, and ultimate scale-down. We took care to seek out stakeholders who would have different perspectives, interviewing UW managers, ECI staffers, members of the foundation community and other funders, neighborhood representatives, early childhood service providers, business leaders involved in ECI, government officials, academic experts, and early childhood advocates. The list of interviewees grew over the course of the project as we gained knowledge about ECI and as early interviewees recommended others for us to interview. We were satisfied that we had interviewed the great majority of key stakeholders and decisionmakers when the names we were given were those of people we had already interviewed. Virtually all targeted interviewees (or alternative representatives of their organizations) agreed to be interviewed.

We cannot publish the list of those interviewed, because interviewees were promised anonymity in order to encourage frankness. Many individuals involved with ECI, however, are necessarily named in this report in order to tell ECI's story. To the extent that we have named individuals, we have done so only when discussing information that is widely known. Names are not attached to confidential information provided during the interviews.[3]

It is always possible, of course, that failing memories might undermine the reliability of interview data, particularly when interviewees have a strong incentive to tell the story in terms most favorable to them. Fortunately, direct factual disputes among interviewees were rare, even when interviewees had quite different perspectives on ECI's problems. Nevertheless, documentary records were essential for resolving factual disagreements and verifying information about ECI's history.

Our second major research task involved obtaining and examining a substantial number of ECI's documentary records, including business plans, enrollment records, and financial records. Whenever possible, we used documentary records to confirm dates, verify enrollment, and assess costs. In addition, documents produced during ECI's planning process helped us understand the initiative's conception, vision, and goals. Finally, the original business plan and the revised plans articulated ECI's intended implementation process.

---

[3]The great majority of interviews were conducted face-to-face, usually at the office of the interviewee and occasionally at the RAND office in Pittsburgh. A few interviews were conducted by telephone (typically for interviewees outside the Pittsburgh region). Interviews were semi-structured: We created interview protocols for several different classes of stakeholders (e.g., funders, neighborhood leaders, ECE providers, UW staff), modifying the protocols for the specific circumstances of each interviewee. Interviews typically lasted 60 to 120 minutes, but some lasted several hours over multiple interview sessions. Because we knew that many of the interviews would raise sensitive topics, we chose not to tape them, to avoid any possible discouragement of open discussion. Instead, we brought a laptop to each interview and took careful notes. Interviews were typically conducted by two RAND researchers, but sometimes three RAND researchers were present and sometimes only one.

As with the interviews, our aim in gathering documents was comprehensiveness: We sought all of ECI's central records on enrollment and costs, all of its proposed and approved business plans, any documents describing its organizational structure, and early concept papers articulating its original vision. We had no difficulty finding business plans and conceptual documents, but available data on costs and enrollment were not complete.[4] As a result, it was impossible to break down costs into finer classifications than those we discuss in Chapters Three through Five; we also had to make some minor assumptions to fill in gaps in the data. These assumptions are discussed in the Appendix. Although more-complete financial and enrollment data would permit a more finely grained analysis, we do not believe that our conclusions would be substantially changed by such an analysis.

Third, we constructed quantitative models to analyze cost and enrollment data and to understand how and why actual figures deviated from ECI's original plans. We reconstructed the model that ECI's planners used for the original business plan, and we then simulated modifications of the plan based on changes in two assumptions that contributed to the plan's underestimation of ECI's costs. This permitted us to estimate the relative contribution of several different factors to ECI's costs (reported in Chapter Five). The cost models are described in detail in the Appendix.

Throughout the study, our analysis was informed by existing empirical literature. Our literature review focused on ECE but also included studies related to welfare reform and community-based social interventions. That literature is cited throughout this report; the References provides a complete list.

After completing the bulk of our analysis, we presented our preliminary findings to several small groups of key stakeholders representing the major constituencies involved in ECI. These formative briefings provided the opportunity to check our findings for factual errors and interpretive nuances. This report sums up the findings that followed from the interviews, document review, cost modeling, and

---

[4]It is possible that some of ECI's records were lost in the transfer from UW to the University of Pittsburgh in 2001. It is also possible, however, that UW never had very good records on ECI, particularly on the allocation of costs.

literature review, with refinements from the subsequent feedback received in the formative briefings.

Before beginning the main analytic tasks of the report, we devote the next two sections of this chapter to critical background information, describing both the motivations that led to the creation of ECI and the obstacles that it had to surmount.

THE IMPORTANCE OF QUALITY IN EARLY CARE AND EDUCATION

The primary initial motivator for ECI's planners was the belief that high-quality ECE services would improve a variety of long-term developmental, educational, and social outcomes for the children served and, ultimately, for the children's communities and the society at large.

For ECI, *high-quality* generally meant adherence to standards set by NAEYC, the premier membership organization for researchers and practitioners in the ECE field.[5] NAEYC standards require high staff-to-child ratios, small group sizes, highly trained staff, and developmentally appropriate play and instructional activities, toys, and other materials. These standards are similar to federal requirements for Head Start centers but have higher requirements in certain areas, such as minimum staff qualifications. To support high staff qualifications, ECI aimed to raise the level of compensation for ECE provider staff, who are typically paid low wages and often lack health benefits. In addition, unlike NAEYC or Head Start, ECI imposed a rigorous quality monitoring system.

ECI planners expected that about 70 percent of children would receive these services in classroom settings on a part-day basis (generally 3 to 3.5 hours daily) for five days a week. The remainder would receive them in either a child-care center or a family child-care home setting for a full day (approximately 9 hours) of combined education and child care. Thus, ECI was to be both "education" and "child care," but education was its main focus. To a lesser extent,

---

[5]ECI standards for family child-care homes were based on standards set by the National Association for Family Child Care (NAFCC), which are quite similar to NAEYC standards but tailored to the home environment.

planners envisioned providing some health care and nutrition (i.e., breakfast and/or lunch) services to children in ECI classrooms and centers, also much like Head Start. In addition, ECI required some level of parent participation, an element common to most high-quality ECE programs.

ECI's planners were aware of a growing body of research suggesting that intensive, high-quality ECE programs can improve cognitive and developmental outcomes for children, especially children with developmental delays or from low-income families. This research is based on several different ECE programs launched since the 1960s (see Reynolds, 2000; Campbell et al., 2001; Karoly et al., 1998; Guralnick, 1997; Barnett, 1995; Yoshikawa, 1995; and Schweinhart, Barnes, and Weikart, 1993). While the specifics varied among the programs studied, all of the programs provided intensive, developmentally appropriate play and instruction (on either a half-day or a full-day basis) by highly trained staff. Most also required some amount of parent participation. To assess impacts on children over time, some of the interventions randomly assigned children to treatment and control groups; in other cases, evaluators established matched comparison groups to estimate program effects.[6] Evaluation results generally indicate that these kinds of interventions can produce short-term improvements in cognitive abilities, as well as short- and long-term gains in social and educational outcomes (i.e., reduced grade retention, fewer special education referrals, higher test scores in reading and math, and higher graduation rates) (Reynolds et al., 2001; Reynolds, 2000; Campbell et al., 2001; Campbell et al., 2002; Karoly et al., 1998; Guralnick, 1997; Barnett, 1995; Yoshikawa, 1995; and Schweinhart, Barnes, and Weikart, 1993). A few studies have followed participants beyond high school and found long-term positive impacts on several adult measures, including higher earnings, reductions in welfare recipiency, and reductions in criminal behavior (Campbell et al., 2001; Campbell et al., 2002; Schweinhart, Barnes, and Weikart, 1993).[7] Many of these results were widely known in the

---

[6]In both experimental and matched studies, the comparison groups included children in a variety of child-care settings (including some children cared for at home by parents). The studies were designed to compare the effect of a specific ECE program with that of any alternative in which the child would otherwise spend his or her time.

[7]For a good review of the literature, see Reynolds, 2000.

mid-1990s, when ECI was planned, and more-recent studies have confirmed favorable long-term findings.[8]

Moreover, there is some evidence that the benefits of these programs to government and society outweigh their costs. The first systematic study to document such benefits was conducted by evaluators of the High/Scope Perry Preschool Project, an intensive half-day demonstration program (supplemented by weekly home visits) for three- and four-year-old children that was implemented in Ypsilanti, Michigan, in 1962 (Schweinhart, Barnes, and Weikart, 1993). The researchers used a prospective experimental design (with random assignment to treatment and control groups) to follow 58 children who had participated in the program and 65 children who had not. In comparison to the control groups, at age 27, a substantially higher proportion of program participants had graduated from high school, and much lower proportions of participants had been placed in special education classes, had been on welfare as adults, or had committed a crime. Program participants also had significantly higher earnings than controls did on average.[9]

Based on these results, the researchers estimated that each $1 spent yielded more than $8 in benefits to program participants, government, and society (just over $7 in benefits to government and society alone) (Schweinhart, Barnes, and Weikart, 1993). A majority of these benefits (65 percent) were in the form of cost savings to society resulting from a reduction in crime. Another 28 percent of the benefits were in the form of higher income for program participants (net of reductions in welfare payments) and the resulting higher tax revenues for government. During the early planning and fundraising phases of ECI, planners and advocates cited this study most fre-

---

[8]ECI's planners may have overestimated the extent to which research has demonstrated which specific components of high-quality ECE lead to improved outcomes for children. The evaluations described above cannot determine the specific dimensions of a program that were necessary for it to produce its favorable results. In consequence, even today, considerable uncertainty remains regarding the specific determinants of favorable child-welfare outcomes in ECE programs (see Blau, 2001; National Research Council, 2001).

[9]All of these differences were statistically significant. Differences between program participants and controls on other measures, such as IQ and number of years retained in grade, were no longer statistically significant at age 27 (Schweinhart, Barnes, and Weikart, 1993).

quently when arguing that ECI was a highly cost-effective investment for Allegheny County and the state. More recently, a new analysis of the results of the Perry Preschool Project (Karoly et al., 1998) used a more-conservative benefit-cost methodology and still found the program to be very cost-effective, producing over \$4 in total savings per \$1 of program costs.[10] The researchers further concluded that such programs have the greatest potential to achieve net cost savings when, like ECI, they are targeted to disadvantaged children (i.e., those experiencing such stressors as poverty or poor nutrition).

In addition to the experimental research on model programs, nonexperimental studies of the effects of different child-care arrangements on child development have generally found that child-care programs operating at a high level of quality tend to produce better social, cognitive, and educational outcomes for children than do those assessed as low quality (Helburn, 1995; Howes, 1997; Howes et al., 1998; National Research Council, 2001; NICHD, 1999; NICHD, 2000; Peisner-Feinberg and Burchinal, 1997; Peisner-Feinberg et al., 1999; Ruopp et al., 1979; Vandell and Wolfe, 2000). The high-quality centers examined in these studies had high staff-to-child ratios, small group sizes, well-trained staff, and experienced directors, and they employed developmentally appropriate activities. In the case of family child-care homes, the research suggests that the provider's level of education or training is the most important determinant of quality and is likely to have the most influence on child outcomes (Helburn and Bergmann, 2002; Vandell and Wolfe, 2000).[11]

---

[10]As the researchers noted, this is a conservative estimate in that some likely benefits were excluded from the analysis, either because they were not measured (e.g., benefits for parents) or could not easily be monetized (e.g., avoidance of pain and suffering among people who would be crime victims in the absence of the program) (Karoly et al., 1998).

[11]As already mentioned, however, the research literature tells little about the relative importance of each of these structural characteristics. For example, no one knows what the incremental impact of higher staff-to-child ratios is on child outcomes versus, say, the incremental impact of improved staff education. For a discussion of this issue, see Blau, 2001, and National Research Council, 2001.

THE "NOBLE BET"

Although ECI wanted to replicate the high quality of service and the long-term child welfare benefits of earlier ECE programs such as Perry Preschool, it went well beyond such programs in three important respects, making it uniquely ambitious:

- ECI aimed to provide high-quality ECE services not on a small, experimental scale in a demonstration program, but for large numbers of low-income children (7,600, representing nearly 80 percent of the targeted "unserved" population) throughout Allegheny County.

- ECI made community control an essential element of the initiative, believing that success on a large scale required that each neighborhood have substantial autonomy to define its needs and operate its services.

- Finally, and perhaps most ambitiously, ECI aimed to change public policy, persuading the state to devote substantial additional public resources to ECE and to accept responsibility for ECI's funding in the long term, thereby ensuring its sustainability.

Indeed, although ECI's planners recognized that the initiative's countywide scope made it more ambitious than previous efforts, they may have underestimated the extent to which the initiative would be exploring new ground. ECI did not include a pilot or demonstration period in a small number of neighborhoods, because the planners believed that Perry Preschool and similar programs had already demonstrated the viability and value of high-quality ECE on a small scale. But ECI's goals went far beyond anything attempted in the Perry Preschool and other experimental programs. Head Start, of course, is a nationwide ECE program that seeks to provide high-quality ECE services, but it serves a relatively small proportion of eligible children in most communities, and most experts believe that its quality varies widely across providers (U.S. General Accounting Office, 1997; Zigler and Muenchow, 1992). ECI had much the same goals as Head Start but intended to address Head Start's weaknesses in both participation rates (by providing sufficient funding and neighborhood involvement to ensure the enrollment of a high proportion of eligible children) and consistency of quality (by including a rigorous system of quality monitoring). Its challenges were fundamentally different from and greater than those facing a small-scale, clearly defined, experimental program such as Perry Preschool.

In addition to having ambitious goals, ECI faced enormous political, institutional, economic, and cultural obstacles. These included pervasive low quality among many of the existing child-care providers (reflecting in part the low market wages for child-care workers), political ambivalence about the appropriate public role in ECE, an underappreciation of the benefits of quality (by many policymakers and parents alike), wide variations in physical and organizational resources in low-income neighborhoods, and the challenges of building a large, new initiative from scratch.[12] An early supporter of ECI in the business community described ECI publicly as a "noble bet."[13] In our view, that description is quite appropriate. ECI's goals were noble, but their achievement would be difficult and required a calculated gamble. Indeed, to have achieved all of ECI's aims would have been a heroic feat.

The implication is this: *Given the scope of the aims and the scope of the obstacles, success required that ECI have a clear sense of market realities in early care and education, a well-designed theory of action, an effective strategy for inducing a commitment of public funding, and a coherent organizational structure.* In Chapters Three through Six, we explain how weaknesses in these areas undermined ECI's success. That analysis is preceded, in Chapter Two, by a brief history of ECI that may be of interest not only to those unfamiliar with the initiative, but also to stakeholders who may wish to re-examine ECI from a bird's-eye perspective. Chapter Seven concludes the report with lessons for the future, including public-policy implications.

Before proceeding, however, it is useful to summarize the extent to which ECI succeeded or failed in achieving each of its key goals.

---

[12]See Blau, 2001, and Gormley, 1995, for more detailed discussions of some of these issues.

[13]The term was coined by Charles J. Queenan, Jr., a prominent Pittsburgh attorney.

THE BOTTOM LINE

ECI was a complicated endeavor with many facets, so any summary necessarily simplifies and omits issues. This report, in its entirety, provides a lengthy discussion of ECI's performance; the following provides a summary of ECI's record in achieving its goals.

Quality

Evaluating quality of service and child welfare outcomes was not part of RAND's charge and falls outside the scope of this report. Quality of service and child welfare outcomes are being examined by the SPECS (Scaling Progress in Early Childhood Settings) group, a research team from the University of Pittsburgh and Children's Hospital in Pittsburgh. RAND did not review the SPECS methods, so we simply note the findings to date of the SPECS team here. According to the SPECS report (Bagnato, 2002), ECI succeeded in promoting quality in participating ECE programs and favorable outcomes for participating children. More specifically, the report states that ECI children demonstrated effective social and behavioral skills and went on to succeed in kindergarten and first grade, as measured by low rates of grade retention and referral to special education.[14] The findings reported by the SPECS team are substantially what ECI's planners aimed to achieve for participating children.

Although ECI may have succeeded in its goal of promoting high-quality ECE programs, it was far less successful in achieving its other goals (those examined in our evaluation), as we discuss next.

Scale

ECI fell far short of its aims in terms of the number of children participating. The initiative served only about 680 children at its peak, around May 2000.[15] This is only one-quarter of the number expected

---

[14]See Bagnato, 2002, for detailed descriptions of results related to program quality and outcomes for children. Our evaluation addressed separate issues, and our conclusions therefore do not depend on the findings of the SPECS evaluation.

[15]The SPECS study reports a larger number because it counts the cumulative number of children served by ECI over time (1,140 as of October 2000) (Bagnato, 2002). The

to be served at that point in time and less than one-tenth of the total number targeted for service.

If measured in terms of the total number of hours of service provided, ECI's achievement still falls short, but less dramatically so. The original business plan assumed that 71 percent of ECI children would be in part-day programs; in fact, nearly 100 percent of ECI children were in full-day programs. The average number of hours of service per child was therefore far higher than expected. While ECI served fewer children than intended, it provided more-intensive service for each child. Even accounting for this difference, however, ECI at its peak was providing only about half as many hours of service as the original business plan had intended for that point in time.[16]

Partly because the service was more intensive than planned, costs per child were substantially higher than expected. In 1999 (year three of implementation), ECI's cost averaged $13,612 per child-year.[17] Although this is not dramatically different from the cost of other, widely cited high-quality ECE interventions,[18] it is three times as high as the cost expected in the original business plan ($4,407). In Chapters Three through Five we explore a number of reasons for the disparity between expected and actual cost. Here we mention three prominent reasons. First, the shift from (largely) part-day services to full-day services raised per-child costs dramatically. Second, the plan assumed that operational cost per child was the same at all levels of enrollment, failing to recognize that cost per child is inevitably substantially higher in providers that are less than 100 percent enrolled. Third, ECI's plan required a substantial bureaucratic structure both centrally and at the neighborhood level,

---

peak number served is more relevant to our study, however, because ECI's scale goals were defined in terms of enrollment achieved at specific points in time, rather than the cumulative number of children served.

[16]We estimate that ECI was providing about 34,000 child-hours of service per week in May 2000, compared to about 73,000 child-hours per week expected by then in the original plan.

[17]1999 was the last full year of ECI's full-scale operation (as well as the last year for which we were able to obtain financial data). Details on the methodology and assumptions for calculating costs are provided in the Appendix.

[18]For example, the High/Scope Perry Preschool Project cost an estimated $12,148 per child (in 1996 dollars) (Karoly et al., 1998).

and it was unduly optimistic about the administrative costs associated with this structure.

Community

ECI's community-driven strategy had some successes and a number of failures. Devolution of authority to the neighborhood level succeeded in a few neighborhoods (most prominently, Braddock and Wilkinsburg) where local leaders eagerly joined the ECI process and established plans that led to a strong working relationship with ECI management (ECIM) and, ultimately, the creation of new, high-quality ECE programs operated by neighborhood-based agencies. Moreover, community leaders in a number of neighborhoods affected by ECI joined together to establish an ongoing support and advocacy network for early childhood and school readiness issues.

But disappointment is widespread in many of the neighborhoods that were targeted by ECI. Some local leaders felt that ECI did not live up to its promise of permitting neighborhoods to define their needs and the ECE services they wanted. In their view, ECI's process for approving neighborhood plans imposed unreasonable delays, and ECI imposed a narrow definition of quality that precluded much local discretion. This left substantial resentment in some neighborhoods, especially those that did not get an early start in the process and were eventually cut off when ECI was scaled down in 2000. Even in neighborhoods that successfully launched ECE programs under ECI's sponsorship, lead agencies felt undermined in 1999 and 2000 when ECI's ground rules were in flux. A number of lead agency staff expressed frustration at their inability to get consistent policy answers during this period.

Sustainability

Although ECI helped to raise the profile of ECE as an important policy issue in communities around Pennsylvania and in state government, it failed in its explicit goal of achieving a state commitment to support the initiative with public funds.

Privately funded initiatives to promote high-quality ECE are now operating in several other communities in the state, including

Philadelphia and York; ECI was the first of such efforts, and the publicity it achieved likely helped to promote similar initiatives elsewhere. ECI attracted the attention of important business leaders, first in Allegheny County and later statewide, and the efforts of such leaders have helped to give ECE a more important (if still limited) role in the agenda of state government in Pennsylvania.

But ECI's lobbying efforts with the governor, the secretary of public welfare, and other state officials did not produce a commitment to provide public support for the continuing operation of the initiative, which has now scaled back to include only two of the original neighborhood agencies, serving approximately 300 children.

The inability to garner a commitment from the state was apparent relatively early. At UW, some of those responsible for supervising ECI recognized that sustainability would have to be achieved by other means and sought to make changes in the initiative to make better use of existing state funding streams. This effort was only partly successful, and it led to a power struggle over the direction of ECI as well as to frustration and resentment in the neighborhoods. Sustainability of the two remaining neighborhood agencies supported by ECI has not yet been demonstrated and will be a major goal for these two agencies over the next three years while their foundation funding continues.

Positive Aspects of ECI's Legacy

Although ECI failed to achieve its greatest ambitions, its legacy is not entirely negative. ECI succeeded, first of all, in building the capacity of a number of low-income neighborhoods to provide ECE services that apparently are of high quality. In the economically depressed suburb of Braddock, for example, not a single licensed day-care center was operating prior to the arrival of ECI. ECI's lead agency in Braddock now supervises the operation of five licensed centers, established through the support of ECI, in Braddock and the surrounding neighborhoods. The value of those services is suggested by the favorable results that the SPECS team reports for ECI children.

ECI also succeeded in helping a number of Head Start providers to improve their programs. Traditionally, Head Start offers a part-day program, an average of 3.5 hours per day for most providers in

Allegheny County. A number of Head Start providers were interested in expanding their service to include full-day, "wrap-around" care. Prior to ECI, no Head Start programs in Allegheny County were licensed by the state to offer care and receive state subsidies. ECI funds and technical assistance were used to achieve licensing and to add wrap-around care in 20 Head Start programs serving over 300 children.

The attention that ECI drew to the importance of quality not only contributed to the creation of similar initiatives elsewhere in the state, but also reportedly motivated improvements in the quality of several major nonparticipating child-care centers around Allegheny County. Some have become accredited with NAEYC and others are moving toward accreditation.

In addition, ECI demonstrated the ability of the Pittsburgh community to mobilize large-scale support and funding from diverse constituencies and political perspectives. The mere fact that ECI was launched is a testament to the imagination, motivation, and collegiality of leaders in the Pittsburgh region, from the foundations to the business community to the neighborhoods. Many communities could not have organized and launched such an ambitious initiative; the fact that Pittsburgh could do so suggests promise for bold plans in the future (with, one hopes, better design and execution).

Finally, ECI's troubles may ultimately serve a useful purpose by illuminating the serious public-policy dilemmas associated with ECE. Public policy in Pennsylvania and across the United States is profoundly ambivalent about the appropriate role of government in the care and education of children younger than school age. ECI's failures were partly attributable to conflicting values related to the developmental needs of children, on one hand, and incentives for parents to work, on the other. The public policies of states and the federal government have not yet resolved these tensions. In the final chapter of this report, we explore some of the public-policy challenges associated with ECE.

Chapter Two

A BRIEF HISTORY OF THE EARLY CHILDHOOD INITIATIVE

This chapter provides a narrative history of ECI from the time it was first conceived through the 18-month planning period that led to its launch at UW in 1996, the creation of plans in participating neighborhoods, the implementation of ECE services, and the initiative's ultimate scale-down in 2000. The narrative is derived both from an extensive examination of ECI's documentary archives and from our interviews with stakeholders on all sides. It chronicles the major steps in planning ECI, identifies the key individuals involved in planning and implementation, summarizes the original business plan and the two revisions that followed, discusses experiences in a number of neighborhoods, and describes the identification of implementation problems and responses to those problems. For readers unfamiliar with ECI, this chapter provides useful background information that should make it easier to follow the analysis in Chapters Three through Six. For ECI's stakeholders, who are familiar with much of the story, this narrative may help to clarify ECI's history from a global, retrospective perspective.

Before beginning the narrative history, we present, in Figure 2.1, a rough timeline of some of the key events in ECI's history. Readers may wish to use this timeline as a reference throughout the report.

GENESIS

The original inspiration for a major ECE initiative in the Pittsburgh region came in the fall of 1994 from Margaret Petruska, then director

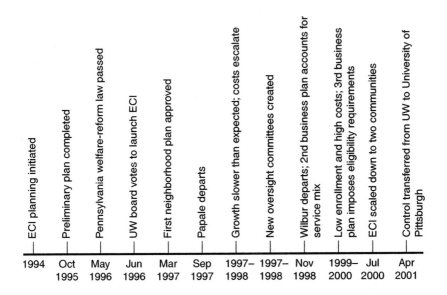

Figure 2.1—Timeline of Key Events

of programs in health and human services at the Heinz Endowments.[1] After years of funding local demonstration projects in child care and early education, Petruska decided that Allegheny County needed a large-scale effort to expand ECE services for low-income, at-risk children. She discussed the idea with two people with whom she had worked in the past and who she believed could provide useful input and criticism. One was Victor Papale, then vice president for resource management at the UW of Allegheny County. Papale had much experience working with UW-funded community agencies and service providers. He also had considerable program administration experience, having previously served as administrator for two different county agencies. The second person was Jerlean Daniel, professor of child development at the University of Pittsburgh and a highly regarded expert in child development who was at the time

---

[1]The reconstruction of the genesis and initiation of ECI relies on information derived from our interviews with various stakeholders, as well as on the transcript of a meeting held between a group of the original planners and staff at the University of Pittsburgh's Office of Child Development in the fall of 1996. The purpose of the meeting was to document the details of how ECI was conceived and planned.

president of the National Association for the Education of Young Children (NAEYC). Papale and Daniel supported and helped to refine the idea of establishing a large-scale ECE initiative for Allegheny County.

The early planners felt such an effort was needed for two primary reasons. First, small-scale programs in Allegheny County had been insufficient to reach substantial numbers of disadvantaged children, and there were significant gaps in the systems of existing services. In 1994, a study conducted by the University of Pittsburgh's Office of Child Development identified over 18,000 children under age six in Allegheny County who were living in poverty (Farber, Williams, and Groark, 1994). A significant number of these children had been born to teenage mothers, were low-birthweight babies, or had received late prenatal care. Yet the University of Pittsburgh researchers estimated that only about 43 percent of these children were receiving any kind of family support, subsidized child care, or publicly funded early education services (Farber, Williams, and Groark, 1994).

Second, ECI's initiators were impressed by the growing body of research indicating that high-quality ECE services lead to improved school performance and other long-term gains such as a reduced likelihood of juvenile delinquency. As noted in Chapter One, *high-quality* services are usually defined as those with developmentally appropriate curricula and play activities (i.e., activities tailored to the developmental capabilities of each child) and a high degree of parent involvement; they are generally expected to include structural elements such as small group sizes, high staff-to-child ratios, and a highly trained staff (see, e.g., Gormley, 1995).

The planners envisioned an initiative that would break new ground by implementing high-quality ECE on a large, countywide scale. In addition, they agreed that such an initiative should, to the extent possible, be community driven. In other words, neighborhoods should be given considerable discretion over the design and administration of their own high-quality ECE programs. Other initiatives to improve services in low-income communities in Allegheny County (such as the New Futures initiative of the Annie E. Casey Foundation) had met with resistance or ended in failure, and many of those involved believed that a lack of sufficient community input was a major source of the problems. Moreover, among foundation staff and social service planners across the nation, there was (and continues to be) a growing interest in pursuing social interventions that are community based or community driven (see, e.g., Center for the Study of Social Policy, 1996; Schorr, 1997; and Zigler, Kagan, and Hall, 1996).

Petruska also consulted Robert Haigh in the Pennsylvania Department of Public Welfare (DPW) to get a sense of whether the state might commit funding to a large-scale ECE effort. Haigh had worked for several years in state government, and part of his job was to be a liaison between Pennsylvania foundations and DPW. Although he made no guarantees, he told Petruska that state policymakers might eventually be persuaded to support ECI with state funds if it could demonstrate favorable results for children.

The planners' hopes about the prospect of getting state support were encouraged by the growing interest throughout the country in raising the quality of ECE programs, especially for at-risk children. Fueling this interest was recent research revealing the strong influence of early brain development on children's abilities to achieve in school and as adults (see, e.g., Carnegie Corporation, 1994). This growing body of knowledge, combined with the research suggesting that high-quality ECE programs can significantly improve the school readiness and social development of young children, motivated policymakers in several states to begin investing more in early education programs. ECI's planners could see the growing interest in ECE among policymakers across the country and were optimistic that Pennsylvania would join the other states that were increasing their investments.[2]

The planners agreed that UW was an appropriate organization to launch ECI and house it temporarily until a more permanent home could be found. Although they recognized that UW did not have extensive experience in the direct operation of large-scale programs, the organization was well known and highly regarded within the

---

[2]Across the country, public funding for ECE continued to increase through the late 1990s. Between 1998 and 2000, overall state spending on ECE programs (including family support programs) for preschool-age children (ages three and four) increased from $1.7 billion to $2.1 billion. Over the same period, state spending on programs for infants and toddlers climbed from $108 million to $226 million (National Center for Children in Poverty, 2000).

community and had the capability to raise the large amount of money that would be needed. In addition, the planners thought that ECE providers would see UW as a neutral agency. Moreover, there was no other obvious candidate to launch the initiative. Enlisting the support of UW Executive Director William Meyer and Heinz Endowments President Frank Tugwell, the planners convinced the boards of both the Heinz Endowments and UW of the importance of ECI. In October 1994, the Heinz Endowments board of trustees agreed to give the UW a $1 million "challenge grant" to begin the ECI planning phase. Four months later, the full UW board agreed to begin the planning process.

THE PLANNING PERIOD

An 18-month planning process ensued. Based on the research that had been conducted by the University of Pittsburgh's Office of Child Development (Farber, Williams, and Groark, 1994) and on indicators of child well-being developed by the Annie E. Casey Foundation, planners identified 80 county neighborhoods with high rates of poverty and unemployment, large numbers of female-headed families and families receiving public assistance, and large numbers of high school dropouts. UW staff recruited community members from the neighborhoods, ECE providers, other social service providers, and local business leaders (approximately 80 total members) to participate in the planning process, which was led by Jerlean Daniel. The group was divided into various subcommittees, which met regularly from May to October 1995. At the end of this process, Daniel produced a preliminary plan based on the agreed-upon principles of the planning group members. The plan set a target of serving 80 percent of the "unserved" children (as defined in the earlier, University of Pittsburgh study) in the identified neighborhoods, ultimately aiming to reach 7,600 at-risk children.

In February 1996, the UW board accepted the preliminary plan but decided that ECI's feasibility needed to be explored further. The board had three primary concerns. First, could UW raise the requisite funds for ECI without diverting donations from other UW programs?[3] Second, was there a reasonable probability of getting the state to assume funding for ECI after a five-year period? And third, was ECI logistically feasible? That is, could the initiative really be expected to deliver services to 7,600 children in 80 neighborhoods across the county within five years?

UW convened committees of volunteer members from the UW board—including some of the skeptics who had raised questions about feasibility—and ECI consultants to address each concern. Several committees investigated the potential for raising funds from particular sources (corporations, foundations, or individuals); a committee chaired by Richard P. Simmons, chief executive officer (CEO) of Allegheny Technologies, examined the strategy for acquiring state support; and a committee chaired by Charles J. Queenan, Jr., a prominent local attorney, developed a business plan. The business plan committee was charged with estimating how much ECI services would cost, what kinds of ECE services would be provided (e.g., part-day preschool programs, full-day center-based or family child-care programs), who would administer the services, and which neighborhoods and children would be eligible.

The committees met periodically from February through May 1996 and presented their findings and recommendations at a meeting of the full board on June 4, 1996. The committees concluded that the fundraising plan was realistic and that a demonstrably successful initiative could impress state policymakers enough to induce a funding commitment within five years. The business plan, meanwhile, spelled out how high-quality ECE services would be provided to unserved children in distressed neighborhoods. Satisfied with the committees' findings, the UW board, which represented a wide swath of Pittsburgh's corporate leadership, unanimously approved the ECI business plan at the June 4 meeting and agreed to launch the initiative. In our interviews, a few stakeholders told us that they had had serious concerns about ECI (notably the prospects for inducing state buy-in) at the time, but, as friends and colleagues of ECI's planners, had felt pressure not to voice their concerns. In any case, the

---

[3]An earlier study commissioned by UW had concluded that funds could be raised without jeopardizing UW's existing fundraising efforts, but several board members were skeptical of the study's results.

dissenters at this point were few and silent: It was clear that ECI had earned the support of key leaders in the business community.

The public-policy context in which ECI would operate changed substantially just as ECI was launched. One month prior to the UW board's decision to launch ECI, the state of Pennsylvania passed a welfare-to-work law. The federal welfare-reform law was passed shortly thereafter, in August 1996. These laws created major changes to the primary welfare program for Pennsylvania families (Aid to Families with Dependent Children, or AFDC, which became Temporary Assistance for Needy Families, or TANF). Most significantly, the new laws imposed mandatory time limits and work requirements on the receipt of welfare benefits. As we describe later, these would ultimately have implications for ECI.

THE ECI BUSINESS PLAN

The person who took the lead in putting together ECI's original business plan was Martha Isler, who had previously served as director of the Bureau of Child Development Programs at Pennsylvania's DPW and as director of the YWCA's Child Care Partnerships program (which administers state child-care subsidies to low-income parents in Allegheny County and provides other child-care services). Isler first became involved in the ECI planning process in March 1996, when she was retained by UW as a consultant to the project. In developing the plan, Isler worked with Papale and with Queenan and the other business leaders who were volunteer members of the committee. The planners also received pro bono assistance from professionals at McKinsey & Co. and Ernst & Young (who lacked specific experience in the business of ECE but had substantial general expertise in business planning and management).

The business plan set the goals and objectives of ECI, articulating the quality, scale, community, and sustainability aims. In addition, it laid out a specific administrative structure for delivering high-quality ECE services. An ECI management (ECIM) staff, housed within the UW, would have day-to-day management responsibilities. ECIM was to define the standards that would constitute high quality (e.g., minimum training and education requirements for provider staff, maximum staff-to-child ratios, and the kinds of curricula, play activities, and equipment that participating programs must have), create a system for monitoring the quality of existing programs to ensure that they met these standards, oversee the allocation of ECI funds to participating communities, and provide community agencies and providers with technical assistance. ECIM staff were to develop a management information system for tracking enrollment and expenditures, and they were to work with a team of evaluators to monitor the quality of services provided and the outcomes for children and communities.

In the view of the planners, the monitoring system was essential for ensuring the maintenance of high quality across an extensive system of service providers. They believed that state licensing inspections were too infrequent to promote consistent quality. Even the higher standards of NAEYC accreditation did not, in the view of the ECI planners, guarantee that high quality would be maintained once the accreditation process was completed. Regular quality monitoring was intended to ensure that high quality was both achieved and maintained by participating providers.

The business plan also addressed the role of the individual communities. Community groups in the targeted neighborhoods would be invited to convene meetings to begin discussing the kinds of services appropriate for their neighborhoods. These meetings were to be open to the public and to involve as many interested community members or organizations as possible. Groups were to survey residents in their neighborhoods about their needs and preferences for ECE services, and to identify existing providers and other community organizations that could potentially contribute to ECI programs. In addition, each community planning group was expected to draft a service delivery plan. Groups could decide to use existing ECE providers in or near their neighborhoods, to establish new providers, or to rely on a mix of the two. They could also decide on the mix of specific services to offer, based on what parents said they wanted: part-day preschool classes (similar to Head Start), full-day child-care centers, family child-care homes, or early literacy programs.

In addition, community planning groups were expected to identify an organization to serve as "lead agency" for the community. (Lead agencies could be involved in the drafting of community plans.) The lead agency would manage ECI programs at the community level, conduct the first level of quality monitoring, and serve as a fiscal conduit, receiving ECI funds and allocating them to participating providers. Lead agencies could also operate their own ECE programs. In sum, communities were intended to have the authority not only to select the array of services they deemed appropriate locally, but also to have direct operational control over the establishment and operation of ECE services, under the supervision of ECIM.

Operationally, the structure suggested by the plan was as illustrated in Figure 2.2.

The business plan also called for the creation of an ECI advisory board, which was to constitute the volunteer leadership of ECI, to represent the larger community of Allegheny County as a whole. It would be expected to determine the criteria by which to judge community plans, review and suggest revisions to the plans submitted, and recommend plans to the UW executive committee for approval. The advisory board was to consist of UW board members, ECE practitioners, other business leaders, and residents from the targeted communities.

The plan stressed the importance of carefully evaluating the performance of the initiative, as measured not only by service quality, but ultimately by outcomes for children and, secondarily, parents and communities. Staff at McKinsey & Co. developed a list of "key performance indicators" by which ECI should be judged. These included performance targets for children, parents, and communities—for example, a promotion rate of at least 95 percent for former ECI children going from first to second grade, increases in the

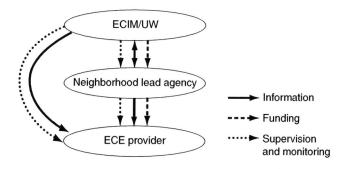

Figure 2.2—ECI's Plan of Operation

amount of educational materials in the home, and increases in the number of accredited centers and family child-care homes. The plan called for hiring an independent research team to conduct the evaluation. Following a competitive bidding process, the SPECS team, consisting of researchers from the University of Pittsburgh and Children's Hospital of Pittsburgh, was ultimately selected (in December 1997). The findings to date of the SPECS team with respect to program quality, community results, and child welfare outcomes are reported in Bagnato, 2002.

The plan concluded that ECI would cost approximately $59 million over five years. This cost estimate was based on a number of assumptions about enrollment rates, administrative costs, and the mix of services that would be chosen by the communities. Different kinds of services in the plan (part-day preschool and early literacy programs, and full-day family and center-based child care) varied in cost from an estimated $1,728 to $8,560 per child per year. The business plan assumed that most of the services would be relatively low-cost, part-day services, and thus that the average cost per child would be $4,000 to $5,000 annually.[4]

The plan also declared that securing state funding to cover most of the costs of the initiative after five years was crucial to the initiative's long-term sustainability. At the insistence of the UW board, the plan included a strategy to phase out the initiative if the state had not made a financial commitment by the end of the third year of implementation (1999). Gradual phase-out would occur over years four and five of implementation: No new children would be enrolled in ECI programs, and those already being served would continue to attend programs only until the end of year five (2001), at which point the initiative would end. Under this phase-out contingency plan, the total five-year cost of the initiative was estimated to be approximately $21 million, or just over a third of the total five-year cost if scale-up were to proceed beyond year three.

---

[4]The lower- and upper-bound costs reported here refer to the total cost per child per year for year three of the initiative, including all capital, operating, and administrative costs. The range of the average cost per child per year reported refers to the five years of the initiative. In our calculations (but not in the original business plan), capital costs were amortized over a 15-year period at a 7 percent discount rate. More details on our cost calculations can be found in the Appendix.

LAUNCH

From June through December 1996, UW staff and ECI consultants worked to get the initiative off the ground. Three people performed much of this work and were regarded as the key staff who would be responsible for operating ECI: Victor Papale, Martha Isler, and Joyce Wilbur, UW vice president for development. Papale had left his staff position at UW in December 1995 and was now serving as a consultant to ECI. Papale and Isler both reported to Joyce Wilbur, who in turn reported to William Meyer, UW CEO. Papale, who had extensive connections with many community groups and agencies throughout the county, especially UW-funded agencies, was responsible for engaging the support and participation of community organizations and existing ECE providers. Isler was in charge of developing eligibility criteria for children and quality standards for ECI programs, writing the Request for Neighborhood Plans (RFNP), overseeing the drafting of a policy and operations manual for lead agencies, establishing provider staff education and training requirements, and supervising the development of a quality monitoring process. Wilbur led the ECI fundraising effort, identifying select groups of local foundations, corporations, and individual UW donors that would be most likely to contribute to ECI and arranging, with the help of UW board members, a variety of fundraising dinners and related events.

The Heinz Endowments and Richard King Mellon Foundation were the first and largest contributors to ECI, committing a total of $22 million ($12 million from Heinz and $10 million from R.K. Mellon). In September 1996, the U.S. Department of Housing and Urban Development (HUD) awarded ECI a $1 million grant to provide ECE services in four local public housing communities.

The UW executive committee and UW staff and consultants identified a group of business leaders, ECE providers, and community leaders to serve on the ECI advisory board. This board met for the first time in October 1996 to begin determining the criteria that community plans would have to meet. For example, plans had to identify existing providers who would participate, identify building space for new programs and provide estimates of renovation costs, identify the number of lead agency and provider staff who would be hired, and estimate the number of infants, toddlers, and preschool-age children who would likely be served. These criteria were finalized by the end of the month, as Isler and Papale were completing the RFNP.

In November 1996, the RFNP was mailed to over 600 community organizations in the 80 targeted neighborhoods. At the same time, UW staff and consultants (primarily Isler and Papale) began holding public meetings at local libraries to spread the word about ECI, persuade community residents and leaders of the importance of high-quality ECE and of the opportunity that ECI represented, answer questions about the RFNP, and encourage community leaders to begin mobilizing residents and convening community meetings.

In the following month, December 1996, UW management hired several staff members who would constitute ECI management (ECIM). These included a director of quality assurance, who was responsible for assisting with the development and implementation of a quality monitoring system; a director of policy and operations, primarily responsible for drafting a policy and operations manual for lead agencies, which would include contracting, budgeting, enrollment, and funding guidelines; and a director of community relations, who was to provide technical assistance to planning groups and lead agencies, mainly by attending community meetings to provide information about the requirements that community plans had to meet. In addition, Papale and Isler provided assistance and information to community groups interested in participating in ECI.

In March 1997, Meyer hired Isler, formerly a consultant to the project, to manage the initiative within ECIM. As ECIM director, Isler oversaw the directors of quality assurance, policy and operations, and community relations. She continued to report to Wilbur, the UW manager responsible for ECIM.

PLANNING IN THE NEIGHBORHOODS

Throughout this time and extending well into the next three years in some communities, community groups and nonprofit agencies in targeted neighborhoods announced and convened public meetings to plan ECI programs. In general, each local planning group included representatives of several contiguous neighborhoods, and each group chose a lead agency to represent these neighborhoods. For example, a planning group in the economically depressed

Monongahela Valley suburb of Braddock included representatives from six neighborhoods: Braddock, North Braddock, East Pittsburgh, Swissvale, Rankin, and the Hawkins Village public housing community (Hawkins Village started with its own community plan and later joined the larger, Braddock-area group). The group elected to have Heritage Health Foundation, Inc., a community foundation in Braddock that had been created through a hospital merger, serve as the lead agency for all six neighborhoods. ECIM allowed local planning groups and lead agencies considerable discretion in defining community boundaries (i.e., in deciding which neighborhoods or municipalities would be included in a given community).

ECIM decided to accept only one service delivery plan from each community. This led to conflict in some communities, as different groups and agencies competed over which would represent the community and submit a community plan. Conflict occurred even in communities where a dominant group and/or lead agency stepped to the fore, as different community leaders advocated their own visions for ECI. Although ECIM community relations staff (two people—the director of community relations and a community outreach specialist who supported the director) attended many of these meetings, informing participants of ECI requirements and answering questions, they generally did not attempt to resolve these conflicts, according to interviewees who attended the meetings. To avoid imposing on the communities' desires, their role was defined primarily in terms of information provision. The community relations staff informed planners about the kinds of services they could choose to offer, the qualifications that ECE program staff and lead agency staff needed, and other ECI requirements.

Each community planning group drafted and distributed surveys to residents to assess their needs for ECE services. The questionnaires generally inquired about number of children, children's ages, current use of ECE services, need for ECE services, and types of services desired (e.g., part-day versus full-day care, evening or nighttime care, and center-based or family child care). According to our interviewees, survey design and administration varied across communities but generally involved informal methods. Some planning groups distributed surveys to parents who happened to attend planning meetings. Others sent teenagers door-to-door to canvass parents. Communities were not expected to use formal procedures, such as drawing a random sample of households to survey. Typically, about one hundred parents completed questionnaires in response to a community survey.

Most local planners were interested in establishing new child-care centers. Planning groups and lead agency staff therefore surveyed their neighborhoods for vacant buildings that might be usable for new ECE programs. Several planners also invited existing providers, both center based and home based, to participate in planning meetings. In some communities, such as the Hill District, existing ECE providers were heavily involved in the planning process and were quite interested in serving ECI children. In others, such as Homewood/East Hills, existing providers were much less involved. (Chapter Four discusses the reasons that existing providers were not more involved in many neighborhoods.) A few existing providers, such as those located in the former mill town of Homestead and the communities of Highlands and Brackenridge, were Head Start centers that were interested in becoming state licensed and adding child-care wrap-around components to their programs, enabling them to offer full-day care.

The first community service delivery plan was submitted to ECIM in early 1997 by a group of residents in a public housing community. The ECI advisory board did not accept it. According to our interviewees, the plan lacked detail in a number of areas, including identification of a lead agency. In fact, the inability to decide on a lead agency proved to be a major problem (among others) in this community. Members of the residents' council were unable to reach consensus on a lead agency and on what types of services should be provided. Two agencies were interested in assuming the lead agency role, and the council was split over which was the better choice. This is an example of the kinds of conflicts within communities that sometimes developed around ECI.

The first community group to receive approval for a service delivery plan was the residents' council at the Hawkins Village public housing community in Rankin (prior to its affiliation with the Braddock-area group). The plan, submitted in February 1997, was developed with assistance from the Allegheny County Housing Authority and from an established ECE provider, Louise Child Care, which the residents' council chose to be the lead agency. Planned services included establishing a new child-care center within the public housing community, as well as recruiting several residents to be family child-care providers. The plan worked its way through the proposal review process the following month, obtaining the approval of ECIM, the ECI advisory board, and, finally, the UW executive committee.

ECIM and UW management were eager to begin providing services in Hawkins Village. Hawkins Village was to be one of the four public housing communities where services were to be funded with the $1 million grant received from HUD in September 1996, and none of that money had been spent yet. ECIM also needed to test its pre-service training curriculum, which had been drafted by a career development committee (consisting mainly of several local academics and ECE practitioners) with assistance from ECIM. Shortly after the plan was approved, a group of residents seeking to become ECI family child-care providers completed the two-week, 50-hour pre-service training program. Trainees learned about ECI policies and procedures; state child-care regulations; best practices for providing learning activities for infants, toddlers, and preschool-age children; and the developmental stages of children in each age group. They also received training in CPR and first aid. The training was provided by a number of different trainers with whom ECIM had contracted, including staff from Louise Child Care.

In addition, ECI staff inspected the apartment of each prospective provider, identifying equipment, materials, and capital improvements that would be needed to meet state regulations and NAFCC standards. After funding improvements in several apartments, ECI began funding operations for these family child-care providers in July 1997. Meanwhile, the lead agency began negotiating with the county's public housing authority to find space for the new center.

QUALITY ASSURANCE

Once a community's plan was approved by ECI, each provider (whether a family child-care provider or a child-care center) had to meet a variety of standards to become eligible for ECI funding. ECI's quality assurance director, working with quality assurance monitors hired by each lead agency, was responsible for ensuring that providers met these standards. Martha Isler also performed a number of inspections. She and her staff were interested, first of all, in whether programs met a basic level of health and safety, such as having smoke detectors installed and stairways with gates to prevent children from falling. To be licensed to operate in Pennsylvania, centers were required by the state to meet these standards and substantially more, including staffing and professional development. In the view of ECIM, the state licensing standards represented a "foundation" for building high-quality services. If programs met these standards, and if program directors and staff expressed an enthusiasm for pursuing NAEYC accreditation and complying with ECI quality standards, they were usually deemed ECI eligible. In practice, most communities decided to establish new providers rather than rely on existing ones. Both new and existing providers were inspected.

Once ECI-eligible, the provider could receive ECI subsidies for eligible children and funding to assist with meeting ECI standards and becoming NAEYC accredited. In general, ECI quality standards were based on NAEYC standards regarding staff-to-child ratios, minimum staff training and education requirements, and curricula. In addition, ECIM expected that lead agencies and providers would attempt to hire staff from within their communities (to ensure the integrity of community control) and conform to a compensation package of pay and benefits that was more generous than the minimal pay and lack of benefits typical in the industry. And in the view of ECI's planners, ECI's most important addition to NAEYC requirements was the ongoing quality monitoring system. The quality assurance director and quality monitors not only inspected prospective providers for their compliance with minimal standards, but also regularly inspected participating providers to ensure that they met the more rigorous standards of ECI and NAEYC.

TRANSITIONS IN ECI MANAGEMENT

Victor Papale left his position as a consultant to ECI in September 1997 in order to be a consultant to another ECE initiative in Colorado. Martha Isler took over most of Papale's work with community planning groups and potential ECI service providers. For ECI, losing Papale meant losing a key link to these agencies.

Approximately five months after Papale left, John Sava, former superintendent of a high-poverty, rural school district, was hired as the UW vice president for early care and education services. Although Sava was not hired specifically to replace Papale, UW management hoped that he could fill the role Papale had previously filled by working closely with community groups and service providers. Sava had a reputation for this kind of work, especially for bringing disparate agencies and constituencies together in support of a common mission.

In January 1998, ECI staff completed their first draft of a policy and operations manual, which was distributed to lead agencies. A further revised version of the manual was given to lead agencies two months later. In February 1998, UW management hired several additional ECI staff. In addition to John Sava, these included a community outreach specialist, who worked with and reported to the community relations director; a family child-care specialist, who provided technical assistance to family child-care providers and reported to the quality assurance director; and a collaboration specialist, who managed contracts with state government and relations with other agencies, such as the YWCA (which administers the state's primary child-care subsidy program).

By the end of the year, ECI was hit with a second key departure. In November 1998, Joyce Wilbur left her position at UW of Allegheny County to take a fundraising position at UW's national office. As a result, Sava assumed a greater role. Isler, who had been reporting to Wilbur, now reported to Sava (who in turn reported to Meyer). The departure of Wilbur left ECI without its key fundraiser and its key intermediary between ECIM and UW management. With Papale and Wilbur out of the picture, Isler was the only one remaining of the three individuals who had been expected to lead ECI's operations.

EARLY PROBLEMS

Physical Infrastructure Challenges

In November 1997, the second community plan, submitted by the Homewood Collaborative community group, was approved. The Collaborative, which represented six neighborhoods in the Homewood/East Hills area of the city of Pittsburgh, planned to establish several new child-care centers and to recruit new family child-care providers. Not long after approval of the plan, ECI staff realized that a lack of code-ready space for new centers in the Homewood area would pose a major challenge. Members of the Collaborative, their selected lead agency (Primary Care Health Services, Inc., a local community health clinic), and ECI staff spent many months trying to identify available space that could be converted to a center at reasonable cost. While family child-care services became operational eight months after plan approval, the first ECI center-based services in the area did not become operational until almost a year and a half after the plan had been approved.

The poor condition of the physical infrastructure in virtually all targeted neighborhoods turned out to be a significant problem for ECIM and local planners. In addition to existing in Homewood, this problem was especially great in the former mill towns of Stowe Township, McKees Rocks (known collectively as Sto-Rox), and Duquesne, and in the Hill District and Oakland neighborhoods in the city of Pittsburgh. Finding adequate space for centers led to delays in getting new services operational. Other factors, such as internal conflicts among community planners, also inhibited programs from getting off the ground in some communities. In some neighborhoods, planned services never became operational.

Expansion of the Committee Oversight Structure

UW management became increasingly concerned with the funding amounts being requested for new child-care centers in response to the facilities problems, as well as with the perceived quality of some of the neighborhood plans. To add an additional layer of quality control to the plan review and approval process, Meyer and the UW executive committee convened a preliminary review committee (PRC) in late 1997. After the ECI advisory board had reviewed and approved a community plan, the PRC would review it; if the committee approved the plan, it would go to the UW executive committee for final approval. The PRC focused on ensuring that community planners had identified space for programs, specified in detail the renovations that would be needed to get the space up to code, and projected how many children they expected to serve and at what cost.

In January 1998, the third community plan was approved, this one for Braddock and several surrounding neighborhoods. In surveying Braddock and its surrounding neighborhoods, local planners found no licensed child-care facilities. Not unlike planners in the other communities, local planners in Braddock hoped to establish several new child-care centers and family day-care homes.

UW management remained concerned about the level of funding being requested in community plans. By early 1998, it had become evident to ECIM and UW staff that all communities were overwhelmingly planning for full-day ECE services. Local planners had found that most parents needed full-day care for their children while they worked. Many of these parents were welfare recipients seeking employment as a result of recently enacted welfare-reform policies (which imposed time limits on benefits). Yet the original business plan had projected that 71 percent of ECI services would be part-day, Head Start–like programs. Full-day, center-based care (with some full-day, family child care) would be much more expensive than Head Start–like programs providing care for 3 to 3.5 hours per day, and these higher costs were reflected in community plans.

In March 1998, unsatisfied that the existing structure was producing well-designed neighborhood plans at a reasonable level of cost, Meyer and the UW executive committee convened an ECI management committee to add another layer of quality control to the community plan review and approval process and to provide ECIM with additional guidance. With this addition, community plans approved by the PRC were vetted further by the ECI management committee before being referred to the UW executive committee. The ECI management committee consisted of three members: Jerlean Daniel, the ECE expert who had been involved in ECI's early planning; James Roddey, a prominent business leader (who was later elected to the office of county executive); and Karen Shapira, a leading philanthropist. The ECI management committee focused largely on reviewing and requesting revisions to community plans.

Neighborhood Planning and Approval Delays

Over the remainder of 1998, several more community plans were approved. But with plans under greater scrutiny, the approval process naturally took longer. For example, local planners in the working-class suburban towns of Stowe Township and McKees Rocks (Sto-Rox) submitted their first formal plan to ECIM in March 1998, after about 15 months of planning. Over the next five months, they were required to revise the plan four times, until the plan was approved in August 1998. Yet ECI services did not become operational in Sto-Rox until 10 months later, in June 1999, when three family child-care providers opened.

The main goal of planners in Sto-Rox was to open an early learning center that not only would provide center-based ECE, but also would offer a variety of additional social services from several community-based providers (Early Head Start services for children under age three, after-school care for school-age children, adult education services, etc.). They spent many months searching for a site for the new center, a difficult task given the quality of the building stock in Sto-Rox. Once a site was identified, local officials told planners that they could not build the center because it could place too much of a burden on the local sewerage system. Planners ended up discarding their plans for the early learning center, eventually finding available space at an existing building (formerly a Catholic elementary school) for a new child-care center. ECI funded renovations to the building during the fall of 1999, and the center opened its doors in December 1999—approximately three years after initial planning had begun in Sto-Rox, 20 months after the first plan had been submitted, and 15 months after plan approval. (And while the center has the capacity to provide ECE services for 54 children, it does not offer the comprehensive set of services that local planners had originally envisioned.) A variety of factors account for Sto-Rox's long road to getting services operational: the lack of available space in the community, zoning problems, and the need to revise the community plan several times in response to the demands of ECIM and the review committees.

The experience of local planners in Sto-Rox was by no means unique. Planners in several other communities, such as Pittsburgh's South Side and the city of Duquesne, experienced many of the same problems in developing community plans that met the approval of ECIM and the review committees, finding adequate space for new centers, and getting programs off the ground. In most communities, these challenges exacerbated the problem of reaching consensus among various constituencies and neighborhood groups.

Nonetheless, throughout 1998, ECI programs became operational in several communities. Some of these were family child-care homes, but most were new centers and classrooms. In Wilkinsburg, a new center opened in late August 1998. Shortly afterward, a new center with the capacity to serve 111 children opened in Braddock. ECI also began to fund renovations to and purchase services from a few existing child-care centers, most notably in the Hill District.

Table 2.1 charts the time from approval to the beginning of operation of centers and family child-care providers. It does not indicate how much time went into the neighborhood planning process prior to ECI's approval of the plan. Systematic data on the time spent in neighborhood planning and negotiation with ECI over the plan, unfortunately, are unavailable for most neighborhoods. Our interviews

Table 2.1

Community Plan Approvals and Program Start Dates

	Plan Approved	Family Child-Care Services Operational	Center Services Operational	Months from Plan Approval to First Children Enrolled
Hawkins Village[a]	March 1997	July 1997	November 2001	4
East Hills/Homewood	November 1997	July 1998	April 1999	8
Braddock	January 1998	March 1998	September 1998	2
Wilkinsburg	March 1998	September 1998	August 1998	5
Hill District	March 1998	April 1999	September 1998	6
Steel Valley	March 1998	NA	June 1998	3
Highlands	August 1998	NA	November 1998	3
Sto-Rox	August 1998	June 1999	December 1999	10
East Liberty	March 1999	NA	July 1999	4
Southside	March 1999	NA	March 2000	12
Duquesne City	March 2000	NA	January 2001	10
Bedford Dwellings	March 2000	NA	May 2001	14

[a]Eventually folded into the Braddock plan.
NOTE: NA = not applicable.

indicate, however, that a number of neighborhoods experienced lengthy periods of community planning and multiple submissions to ECI.

Head Start Initiatives

In addition to its work with community agencies, ECIM provided direct assistance to several Head Start programs in the county that wished to become licensed with the state to offer full-day care and collect state child-care subsidies. In April 1998, ECI received a one-year, $115,000 grant from the state DPW for this purpose. Beginning in mid-1998 and extending into the following year, ECI provided funding and technical assistance to 20 Head Start centers (with a total capacity for just over 300 children) that became licensed.[5]

THE REVISED (1998) BUSINESS PLAN

Concern among ECIM and UW management over higher-than-expected capital and operating costs (resulting from the emphasis on full-day services) ultimately led to the creation of a revised business plan. Work on the plan began in mid-1998 and was completed by November of that year. UW management and ECIM both made significant contributions to the revised plan with help from some of the same staff at Ernst & Young who had assisted with the original business plan.

The revised plan maintained the goal of attempting to serve 7,600 children by the end of year five (2001) and to do so using a community-driven process. But it recognized that the service mix would be drastically different from what had been originally anticipated. Under the revised plan, 95 percent of participating children were expected to enroll in full-day programs, as opposed to the original expectation of 29 percent. Welfare reform was cited as the major reason for this shift in the service mix.

The result was a much larger total projected five-year cost for the initiative: $104 million instead of $59 million. Yet the planners esti-

---

[5]These were in addition to seven new Head Start classrooms (with a capacity to serve 110 children) that were established as part of the community planning process.

mated that about $49 million (47 percent) could be secured through existing state subsidy programs. Pennsylvania has two child-care subsidy programs, both managed by the state DPW. One program, administered in Allegheny County by the YWCA of Greater Pittsburgh (under contract to DPW), provides subsidies for the children of former welfare recipients and the working poor. The other, administered by county assistance offices, subsidizes care for the children of welfare recipients attending workfare or job training or education programs. Pennsylvania had recently begun increasing appropriations for these programs, and there were indications that the appropriations would rise further. To collect this subsidy revenue (which would offset program costs to ECI), the plan stated that all lead agencies would be urged to persuade parents to apply for subsidies and to ensure that as many children as possible were receiving subsidies. (Up to that point, lead agencies had collected very little subsidy revenue.) The remaining $55 million (53 percent) of the total five-year cost was to be covered by the fundraising process already under way. This amount represented only a slight increase over the amount ($51 million) that local, private funders were expected to meet in the original plan.

The revised plan also altered the strategy for securing long-term state funding for ECI. Rather than seek a new line item in the state budget, ECI advocates would attempt to persuade policymakers to raise subsidy reimbursement rates from the current 75 percent to 100 percent of the market rate for care, and preferably to raise them even higher to cover the full cost of high-quality care for subsidy-eligible children. Finally, the plan called for UW to examine progress in February 1999 to determine the extent to which the goals set forth in the revised plan were being met. Most importantly, this analysis would assess the degree to which lead agencies and providers were collecting state subsidy revenue.

FURTHER REASSESSMENT AND REVISION

ECI's Status After Two Years

By the end of 1998 (year two of implementation), eight communities representing 24 neighborhoods had approved community plans. (The plan for one of these communities, Hawkins Village, would eventually become folded into the Braddock plan.) In terms of the number of neighborhoods with approved plans, ECI was slightly ahead of what the original planners had expected (20 neighborhoods by the end of year two). Nevertheless, enrollment was significantly lower than originally projected. ECI served an estimated 233 children in 1998, compared with an original projection of 1,099. Low enrollment reflected many of the problems described above, in particular the time needed to start new services and the difficulties in identifying adequate space for new centers. As a result of these problems, services were not yet operational in all 24 neighborhoods, and several programs had only recently opened.

Fundraising for ECI largely ceased after Wilbur's departure. While ECIM and other UW staff spent some time attempting to raise additional funds (mainly government grants), these efforts did not match the amount of time that Wilbur had spent on this task. UW management felt that large-scale fundraising could not proceed while ECI was far behind its enrollment target. By October 1998, ECI had raised approximately $34 million in donations, grants, and conditional commitments.

In February 1999, UW staff analyzed ECI's progress toward the goals stated in the revised (1998) business plan. The analysis showed that few children were receiving state subsidies; subsidy revenue collected by lead agencies remained negligible—at least in part because the subsidy program was underfunded and parents were subjected to extended time on waiting lists. Subsidy revenue had accounted for only about 5 percent of total ECI program revenues through 1998. Virtually all ECI children were receiving full-day care, and costs per child served were high. In the same month, however, a major policy change infused the state's main child-care subsidy program (which targets former welfare recipients and the working poor) with a substantial funding increase, resulting in shorter waiting lists. Thus, UW management remained hopeful that subsidies could be used to a much greater extent and began to stress the importance of seeking subsidy revenue to lead agencies.

The Third Business Plan

The strong support that ECI had previously held in Pittsburgh's business community began to break down in the face of slower-than-expected enrollment growth and higher-than-expected costs. Concerned about financial trends, the UW board voted on June 15, 1999, to have the business plan revised once again. A detailed draft plan was produced by UW management in July, finalized in early August (with assistance from staff at the consulting firm of Dickerson & Mangus, Ink.), and formally presented to various funders, agency directors, and other stakeholders at an August 2, 1999, meeting at UW. The plan called for (1) involving greater numbers of existing providers with a simplified process for deeming them ECI eligible, (2) prohibiting any new children from enrolling unless their parents had applied for state subsidies, (3) replacing line item funding for lead agencies with funding based on a capitated rate per child enrolled, and (4) aggressively marketing ECI to increase enrollment in ECI programs. The plan also called for the board to delay for one year its decision to either continue or scale down the initiative. Under the original plan, this decision was to be made at the end of 1999 (year three). Under the newly proposed plan, it would be made in November 2000 in order to give ECI, in its revised form, the chance to demonstrate success in reducing costs, increasing enrollment, and persuading the state to raise subsidy rates enough to fund the full cost of high-quality care.

The release of the proposed plan made clear that rifts had opened in the coalition of business leaders, foundations, neighborhood leaders, and ECE advocates that had formed to launch ECI. The proposed plan met with resistance from several directions. One major rift was internal: The plan had been developed without substantial input from ECIM, which was increasingly in conflict with UW management over the direction of the initiative. ECIM and UW management placed different priorities on the initiative's different goals. While maintaining high-quality standards was ECIM's paramount objective, UW management was concerned about enrolling substantial numbers of children at a cost that would permit sustainability. With the initiative short of enrollment targets and costs far higher than expected, the goals held dear by ECIM and UW management seemed to be in tension, putting the leadership at odds. The most important human link between ECIM and UW management had been Wilbur, now departed for the national UW. The disagreements between ECIM and UW management developed into a power struggle for control of the initiative in 1999 and 2000.

Many community stakeholders were also upset with various elements of the plan and felt that they too had been given little opportunity to provide input. Other stakeholders, including the staff at the Heinz Endowments, were equally concerned about the lack of community input.

As a result of these concerns, the UW executive committee agreed to seek community input and further revise the plan. They contracted with Dickerson & Mangus, Ink., a prominent local consulting firm specializing in strategic management and crisis management, to interview a diverse group of stakeholders, including several community leaders. Based on the input provided by this process, UW management (with assistance from Dickerson & Mangus) modified the proposed plan, producing the Year 2000 Revised Business Plan. While differing somewhat from the previous version, the new plan retained most of the earlier version's proposed changes to ECI. In January 2000, the UW executive committee voted to approve the plan. Shortly after approval, UW management and ECIM began to implement elements of the plan while giving lead agencies time to prepare for the remaining program changes.

The most significant change was the mandate that no new children could be enrolled unless their parents had applied for subsidies. Parents of children already enrolled in ECI who had not applied for subsidies were required to do so. Those children already enrolled but deemed to be subsidy-ineligible (i.e., whose applications had been denied) were permitted to remain in ECI under a grandfather clause. UW management instructed all lead agencies to work toward the goal of having at least 90 percent of participating children receiving state subsidies.

Like the plan proposed in July 1999, the 2000 plan called for the replacement of line item funding with funding based on a capitated rate (per child enrolled) and set stringent controls on the extent to which ECI would reimburse lead agencies for administrative expenses. At the request of the lead agencies and ECIM, UW management agreed to delay implementation of capitated funding until July 2000. All told, these were major policy changes for the lead agencies, which struggled to adapt to them.

The 2000 plan also stipulated that no new community plans would be accepted. Review and approval of plans already in the review process were to be completed by the end of June 2000. In addition, at several points throughout 1999 and early 2000, the UW executive committee mandated that no additional children could be enrolled in ECI programs. These decisions were motivated by concern over the initiative's financial sustainability. But the committee later revoked these mandates, usually because lead agencies complained that some centers (especially those that had just recently opened) needed to build up their enrollments to levels approaching their capacity given the fixed costs associated with keeping a center open and staffed.

SCALE-DOWN

An ECI transition committee began meeting on a regular basis in December 1999. This committee consisted of representatives of major ECI funders (including the Heinz Endowments and R.K. Mellon Foundation), top-level UW management, and members of the UW board. The committee's primary objective was to identify an organization that could serve as a new home for ECI. Even before the formation of the committee, UW management had been actively attempting to find an organization that could take over responsibility for ECI.

In the spring of 2000, the ECI transition committee also began to consider scaling the initiative down to a very limited number of communities. ECI reached its peak enrollment in May 2000, serving 686 children—one-fourth the number that the original business plan had expected to serve by that time. (Actual and intended enrollments in ECI are depicted in Figure 2.3.) In June 2000, convinced that ECI was no longer sustainable in its existing form, committee members agreed to convert ECI to a demonstration program, with services provided in just two of the 11 communities with approved plans, Wilkinsburg and Braddock. These sites were chosen because they were considered to be the most successful and enrolled the most children (about 40 percent of the total children enrolled at the time).

The conversion of ECI to a demonstration program serving only Wilkinsburg and Braddock took effect on July 5, 2000. At the same time, UW management laid off most of the ECI staff. UW continued

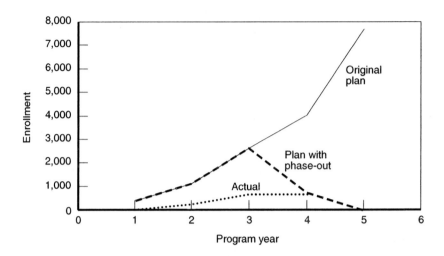

Figure 2.3—Planned and Actual ECI Enrollment over Time

to fund the other nine lead agencies with lesser amounts (approximately $2,500 per child) through the end of 2001. (Some ECI funders agreed to allow their donations to be used for these and other non-ECI early care programs.) UW funding for former ECI agencies for 2002 and beyond is uncertain.

In late 2000, the University of Pittsburgh's Office of Child Development (OCD) agreed to become the new host agency for what is now the ECI Demonstration Program (ECIDP). On April 1, 2001, management of ECIDP was transferred from UW to OCD. OCD receives funding from the Heinz Endowments and R.K. Mellon Foundation for ECIDP and is contracted to manage the two remaining sites for a three-year period, after which they are expected to be self-sustaining. With funding from the two foundations, the SPECS research team continues to track current and former ECI children in Wilkinsburg and Braddock, as well as in the former ECI sites.

CONCLUSION

When ECI was officially launched in the summer of 1996, it included a business plan that had been prepared under the scrutiny of key downtown business leaders and with the assistance of staff from high-powered consulting firms. Despite the scrutiny, however, the business plan had several weaknesses that contributed to ECI's difficulties. These weaknesses were compounded by problems in ECI's operation and implementation. Chapters Three through Six discuss some of the weaknesses in ECI's operational plan, administrative structure, and implementation that contributed to its failure to achieve its goals.

Chapter Three

ECI'S THEORY OF ACTION

Although the motivation for ECI was an accepted body of research demonstrating the long-term benefits of particular kinds of ECE programs, the way in which the initiative was intended to operate was novel in two important ways. First, ECI aimed to create a countywide system of high-quality ECE services rather than just a small-scale pilot program. Second, it aimed to put the various ECE programs under the control of local neighborhood organizations (subject to quality standards enforced by ECI's central administration). At the time of ECI's inception, no models existed of high-quality ECE delivered on a large scale through grassroots, neighborhood control. ECI therefore needed to develop its own "theory of action" to explain how the initiative would work. That theory of action can be found in ECI's original business plan, approved in 1996.

Figure 3.1 depicts ECI's theory of action. The figure incorporates the plan of operation shown in Chapter Two, but expands it to include funders and the ultimate intended beneficiaries of the services, the children and families. In the business plan, ECI's theory of action focused on an extensive list of activities to be conducted by a central administration at UW, consisting of both UW management and ECI management (ECIM), and an additional extensive list of activities to be conducted by lead agencies in each neighborhood. The central administration was expected to supervise the neighborhood lead agencies, and each lead agency was in turn expected to supervise the participating providers in its neighborhood (some of which were directly operated by the lead agencies).

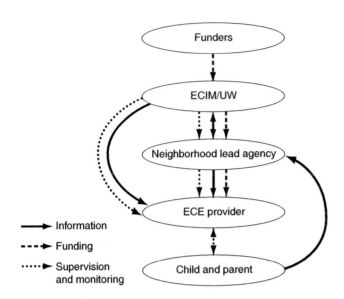

Figure 3.1—ECI's Theory of Action

According to the theory of action, funding would flow down through the structure. Funders would give their money to UW, which (through ECIM) would fund community groups. These in turn would fund providers, which would offer services intended to attract the parents of the children.

Supervision and quality assurance were also designed as top-down processes. The central administration was responsible for approving neighborhood plans and the budget expenditures of lead agencies. The quality of the ECE services provided to children was to be assured through monitoring by both the lead agencies and the central administration.

To implement a system of quality monitoring, standards of quality had to be defined, which was another responsibility of the central administration. Similarly, the central administration was expected to create standards for the operation of lead agencies; these standards were to be defined in a lead agency operations manual.

Meanwhile, lead agencies were responsible not only for managing and monitoring existing child-care centers and family child-care providers participating in ECI, but also for establishing new providers. In some instances, new centers would have to be created from scratch.

Unlike funding, supervision, and monitoring, information was intended to flow upward as well as downward. The business plan expected that parents would inform lead agencies of their needs and desires related to ECE; it required all neighborhood planning groups to conduct surveys of local parents. The neighborhood lead agencies would in turn inform the central administration of neighborhood needs. In the other direction, the central administration was expected to provide information to lead agencies and providers in the form of professional development and technical assistance services.

Perhaps the most important point to notice about Figure 3.1 is this: While most of ECI's theory of action concerned measures to be taken by the central administration and the neighborhood agencies, the ultimate goals of high-quality ECE services for large numbers of children around the county were to be served by the relationship between providers and families. ECI's theory of action created an extensive structure above that relationship rather than addressing it more directly. This put several layers of organization between the funders and the primary intended beneficiaries (i.e., the children to be served) and led to a number of problems in implementation.

The extensive structure implicit in ECI's theory of action is a direct result of the initiative's intent to simultaneously pursue community control and a centrally determined definition of quality. Both of these aims were supportable in themselves. The desire to impose an intensive, centralized system of quality monitoring was motivated by the plausible observation that, given the powerlessness of children in care, pervasive low quality in the child-care industry could be systematically addressed only through regular, rigorous inspections by monitors with a clear understanding of quality. The desire to permit community control was motivated by the knowledge of externally imposed, heavy-handed failures of the past; by the belief that grassroots involvement would promote success in implementation and sustainability; and by the laudable desire to permit those most affected by the initiative to have a substantial role in directing it.

Even though each strategy had merit, pursuing both simultaneously proved to be problematic. The combination not only required the substantial organizational structure illustrated in Figure 3.1, but also created internal conflicts when community desires ran afoul of ECI's definition of quality. We explore these consequences next.

THE ADMINISTRATIVE BURDEN

One consequence of ECI's multilayered theory of action was that each layer of administration added to the cost of the initiative. The original business plan optimistically assumed that the cost of ECI's central administration at UW would amount to $286 per child (or 6.5 percent of a total cost of $4,407 per child) in year three of implementation. In fact, this was a serious underestimate: In year three (1999), central administrative costs were actually $1,231 per child (or 9.0 percent of the total cost of $13,612).[1] Given the extensive array of responsibilities expected of ECIM, the business plan's initial estimate of $286 per child appears exceedingly optimistic.

Indeed, despite the fact that administrative costs were far higher (per child) than expected, ECIM may have lacked the resources to do all of the jobs it was tasked to do. ECIM did not have an especially large number of staff, but they were expected to fulfill a wide variety of responsibilities (as described above) for a large number of neighborhoods, lead agencies, and providers across the county. In addition to losing its key fundraising and community outreach staff, ECI appears to have lacked adequate staff in other areas. ECI had one director of quality assurance who oversaw one center-based specialist and one home-based specialist. These three staff were to inspect and evaluate prospective providers, continually monitor participating providers, and provide training and technical assistance (e.g., recommend equipment and curricula to purchase and help providers find qualified staff). They had to provide this support in over 35

---

[1]Central administrative costs included salaries of ECIM staff, part of the salaries of other UW staff who devoted part of their time to ECI, equipment and occupancy costs for ECIM, and some costs for fundraising and lobbying. Unfortunately, data are not available to distinguish among these individual categories.

neighborhoods, and had great difficulty doing so.[2] Indeed, a number of neighborhood leaders were frustrated by the lack of assistance they received from ECI, a problem that was exacerbated by the fact that ECI was spread thin. For example, before prospective providers could be deemed ECI-eligible, ECIM's small quality assurance staff had to inspect and evaluate them (while also continually monitoring and assisting those already participating). In some cases, according to interviewees, months went by before the evaluators provided feedback. In short: For ECIM to achieve all of its assigned tasks for all of the neighborhoods, lead agencies, and providers seeking to participate in ECI, administrative costs would have had to be even higher than the high costs that were actually experienced.

The available financial data that combine lead agency costs with the direct costs of providing ECE services do not permit us to assess the additional administrative costs at the lead agency level. Nevertheless, it is clear that ECI's theory of action required a substantial administrative structure at the lead agency level. Although we have no way to estimate the magnitude of those costs, it seems likely that they contributed significantly to the total cost of the initiative. For example, consider the fact that ECI targeted 7,600 children in 80 different neighborhoods. If each neighborhood had chosen its own lead agency, each lead agency would have served on average fewer than 100 children. In practice, the initiative was less fragmented, because contiguous neighborhoods often joined together under a single lead agency. Even so, the 686 children who were served by ECI at its peak, in May 2000, were divided among 11 lead agencies, for an average of only 62 children per lead agency (although this number presumably would have grown as lead agencies developed new service providers).

---

[2]Some positions went unfilled either for long periods of time or for the duration of the initiative. The center-based specialist position went unfilled for several months. In addition, ECIM was to have hired at least one full-time inclusion specialist to help providers work with special needs children, including children with behavior problems. (One foundation dedicated its grant specifically for this purpose.) UW never filled this position, despite repeated requests by lead agency and provider staff for assistance with special needs children. (In fact, several ECI programs ended up expelling children with behavior problems. This occurred because staff were unable to control these children's behavior, and because the behavior was then complained about by the parents of other children.)

The major point to be made here is that ECI's theory of action, by simultaneously imposing substantial top-down requirements and creating additional structures in each neighborhood, made high administrative costs inevitable. ECI's theory of action envisioned an operational model that required substantial layers of expensive bureaucracy.

As Chapter Two makes clear, high program costs ultimately played a major role in undermining the initiative's sustainability. Administrative expenses explain only part of ECI's cost problems; we address other cost issues in Chapters Four and Five.

THE TIME NEEDED FOR COMMUNITY-BASED PROCESS

ECI's theory of action involved a hierarchical bureaucracy at the same time it aimed to permit neighborhoods to direct their local programs. So ECI's theory of action not only involved many decisionmaking layers, but also vested substantial authority in a layer that moved slowly. Community consensus building, for all its virtues, cannot be done quickly. This does not imply that neighborhood control was a mistake. Devolution of control and authority to the community level requires a tradeoff: Neighborhood-led programs may be more robust and effective than those imposed from the outside, but the necessity of developing skills, resources, and interest at the neighborhood level means that implementation should not be expected to proceed quickly. ECI's theory of action and its need to show results within three years did not reflect this constraint. ECI's planners failed to appreciate how much time neighborhood groups would need to mobilize, assess residents' needs, identify space for child-care centers, develop detailed proposals, and, especially, establish new ECE programs.

Neighborhoods that successfully identified a lead agency, developed a viable service delivery plan, and became operational usually had well-established agencies that were already leaders in the community and ready to assume the lead agency role. These agencies had well-trained staff with experience in budgeting, hiring, subcontracting, and managing grants. They also tended to have more resources (largely in terms of staff and funding) than did agencies that were less successful.

Nevertheless, all lead agencies, including those that were the most successful, faced significant learning curves. To a large extent, they were starting new child-care and early education programs from scratch, often without experience in the field.[3] To be fully successful, a community-based approach would have required a great deal of technical assistance, which ECIM lacked sufficient resources to provide. ECIM had only two staff who provided general technical assistance and outreach services for all communities.

Some neighborhoods needed assistance not only in the development of service plans and providers, but also in the creation of an initial community consensus. A number of community groups experienced great difficulty getting community stakeholders to reach consensus on a particular plan. In several communities, competing groups fought over the right to be the neighborhood's lead agency. ECIM's approach was to let these conflicts play out on their own, but some conflicts never were resolved. ECIM did not have a team of specialists with experience in community organizing.

Experience with other large-scale, community-based initiatives suggests that such a slow, arduous process is necessary. For example, the Annie E. Casey Foundation's New Futures initiative, one of the most ambitious efforts to improve and expand the delivery of services to at-risk youths, originally had a five-year timeframe (like ECI) (Annie E. Casey Foundation, 1995; Center for the Study of Social Policy, 1995; Walsh, 1998). When they launched the initiative in 1988, New Futures planners hoped to create fundamental changes in the youth services systems in five cities (including Pittsburgh). Most cities sought to implement these changes by reaching consensus across diverse constituencies and by including community groups and their leaders in the planning and administration of new programs. Most New Futures sites did not realize substantial progress toward changing youth services systems and meeting their goals until well after the initial five-year period. Joan Walsh (1998, p. 29)

---

[3]Exceptions include Louise Child Care, initial lead agency for Hawkins Village; the Hill House Association, lead agency in the Hill District; and the Allegheny County Intermediate Unit, lead agency in the Steel Valley and in Highlands. Louise Child Care ran several child-care centers in the county, Hill House was already operating its own child-care center, and the Intermediate Unit was operating several Head Start programs.

noted that "everyone now agrees that expecting large measurable declines in teen pregnancy and school failure in just five years was unrealistic for an experimental, multifront, community-building project like New Futures." The same could be said for ECI's goal of using a community-driven process to serve 7,600 children in 80 neighborhoods in five years—and to demonstrate results to the state in only three years.

Another recent large-scale effort that encountered similar problems was the Carnegie Corporation's Starting Points initiative. Starting Points aimed for "systems change": the creation of new governing and advocacy bodies (in 11 sites, including Pittsburgh) that would either make or advocate policy changes to improve the delivery of social services for at-risk children. Most sites sought to integrate services across a broad spectrum of government agencies and providers and to mobilize community residents behind the efforts. While evaluators identified a number of successful outcomes from Starting Points, they found that the initiative failed to create stronger connections among providers of ECE, child health, and family support services. For funders and policymakers, they advise that "the time frame for [large-scale] initiatives should be commensurate with the size of the goals and the level of change that is contemplated" (National Center for Children in Poverty, 2001, p. 32).

ECI planners were attempting to implement on a large scale the kinds of high-quality ECE interventions that have demonstrated significant and lasting positive outcomes for children (e.g., the Perry Preschool Project). Such a plan in itself was ambitious, but it was made even more ambitious by the addition of a community-driven process that was not a characteristic of the model programs that had inspired ECI planners (nor of the few large-scale ECE programs, such as the Chicago Child-Parent Center program, which is discussed in Chapter Seven).

The existing program that comes closest to ECI's approach of marrying the concepts of high-quality ECE and a community-driven process is Head Start. Head Start involves a significant degree of local decisionmaking, with parents and other community members typically serving on advisory boards and having a voice in program design. Many parents also serve as classroom volunteers and eventually become paid staff.[4]

Nonetheless, Head Start does not require consensus within a community or the identification of a lead agency. While the process for becoming a Head Start grantee is competitive, any organization may submit a proposal, and the federal Administration for Children and Families (ACF) (within the Department of Health and Human Services) applies straightforward guidelines in selecting grantees for specific geographic areas. Thus, agencies do not usually "battle it out" to determine who will be the Head Start provider in a given community. Furthermore, ACF has no expectation that grantees will be representative of the larger community in which they provide services.

COMMUNITY CONTROL VS. QUALITY CONTROL

Many neighborhood leaders felt that there was conflict with ECIM over the control of their efforts. ECI's insistence on its own definition of quality inevitably placed constraints on the degree of freedom to be exercised by communities. Its original business plan did not acknowledge the extent to which quality control and community control might be in tension. When ECI was launched, neighborhoods were told to indulge their biggest dreams; some were disappointed when they found that their dreams were not always consistent with the vision of ECIM.

Our interviews suggest that community representatives had doubts about the way ECIM defined quality. Typically, they did not question the use of NAEYC standards but instead focused on ECI's quality monitoring process. In their view, the way in which ECI operationalized high quality (e.g., with frequent inspections and observations by ECI's quality assurance staff, and with rigid rules about which vendors could be used and about who could be hired, including the requirement that all résumés of prospective employees be approved by ECIM) went too far beyond NAEYC standards. In the perception of

---

[4]Note, however, that it is widely believed that local discretion on certain program parameters accounts for the uneven level of quality that exists across Head Start centers (U.S. General Accounting Office, 1997; Zigler and Muenchow, 1992).

most lead agencies and providers, ECIM and UW were overly rigid in their demands. The original RFNP was vague about ECI's expectations in a number of areas. Community agencies were encouraged to be creative and to plan for the kinds of services their residents wanted. With this encouragement, several community groups spent many months creating service delivery plans that they later had to completely discard or significantly change. This problem was a consequence of ECI's simultaneous pursuit of grassroots, community decisionmaking and its own vision of high-quality ECE.

For example, in Pittsburgh's South Side, local planners spent over a year developing a community plan for four neighborhoods, including two public housing communities. Based on the results of parent surveys, neighborhood planners decided to focus first on establishing centers to serve three- and four-year-old children. When they submitted their plan to ECI (in January 1998), the planners felt confident that ECIM and the review committees would demand few revisions. Given the community-driven approach of ECI, they felt empowered to plan for the kinds of programs they wanted to offer. But ECIM insisted that the two centers include infant/toddler care. ECIM wanted all ECI centers to serve children in all age groups (ages zero to five), so as to provide continuity of care as children got older and so that parents with more than one child would not have to go to two locations. This condition had not been clear to the neighborhood planners in South Side, who had believed they were empowered to define their own needs.

Similar conflicts arose in other communities. In one neighborhood, the planning group hoped to provide ECI services using existing providers. Yet after their plan was approved, ECI staff determined that several providers were supplying such low-quality care that they should not participate.[5] This discouraged local planners, who felt they had been misled about the degree to which they had ownership

---

[5]For existing providers under consideration for participation in ECI, ECIM reviewed the summaries of the state's licensing inspections for the preceding two years. If the summaries showed serious and chronic violations of licensing standards, the provider was given six months to remedy the problem and become eligible for ECI funding for quality supplements. ECIM believed that a provider was unlikely to make the effort to reach ECI's quality standards if it had not shown a commitment to reach the less-stringent licensing standards of the state.

over their ECI plan. To be fair, ECIM had made it clear to all planning groups that not all providers included in a plan would necessarily be deemed ECI eligible. Nevertheless, this is another example that illustrates the inherent tension between ECI's goals of enforcing a specific definition of quality and using a community-driven process.

THE ADMINISTRATIVE STRUCTURE

Most interviewees agreed that UW had little experience in directly operating a large-scale service-delivery initiative such as ECI. UW's primary competence lies in distributing funds, not operating programs. Running an initiative on the scale of ECI was a substantial institutional reach for UW. Nevertheless, UW had a number of advantages, including fundraising capacity and relationships with service providers and community agencies around the county. UW might have been an appropriate place for ECI if a strong administrative structure had been set up for the initiative. Unfortunately, ECI's administrative structure only added to the problems implicit in the theory of action.

The administrative structure within ECIM was relatively straightforward; we do not address it here. The problems in ECI's administrative structure were at the leadership level. Figure 3.2 depicts the intended ECI leadership structure, showing the relationship between ECIM and others at UW. On the administrative side in UW, ECIM reported to Joyce Wilbur, who reported to UW's CEO, William Meyer; Victor Papale served as a consultant. Volunteer leadership was supposed to be provided by the ECI advisory council—a group of business leaders, ECE professionals, and community representatives. In addition, ECI, like UW as a whole, operated under the ultimate supervision of the UW board and its executive committee.

ECI's leadership structure had two weaknesses. First, ECI lacked its own independent board. Second, in practice the organization chart quickly became more complicated than the one just described, as a result of the departure of key administrators and the proliferation of volunteer supervisory committees (which we describe below). Both weaknesses made it difficult for anyone involved with ECI to exercise strong leadership.

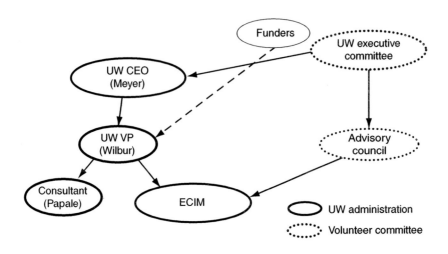

Figure 3.2—Intended ECI Leadership Structure

Absence of a Board

Resolving conflicts about the priority of competing goals requires a strong, empowered, independent board. Unfortunately, UW management itself was confused about authority over ECI, and in particular its relationship to ECI's funders; UW leaders never felt full ownership of ECI and did not perceive that they had the authority to change the business plan. ECI's organizational structure lacked a strong board with both the authority and the stature to clarify the leadership. Although the UW board's executive committee maintained final authority over key decisions, ECI was just one of several matters with which it was concerned; its members lacked the time to provide sufficient oversight.

Confused Authority Lines and Proliferating Committees

The ECI structure became much more complicated than was originally intended. Figure 3.3 is an approximation of the actual leadership structure of ECI as it existed from 1998 to 2000.

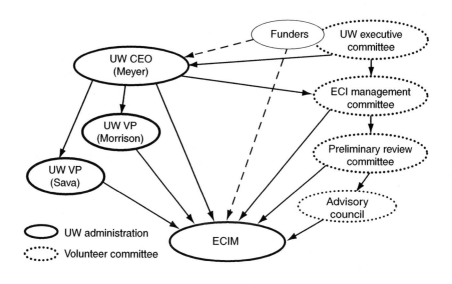

Figure 3.3—Actual ECI Leadership Structure, 1998–2000

On the administrative side, Victor Papale departed relatively early, and Joyce Wilbur left midway through year two of implementation (in July 1998). These were critical departures, because Papale and Wilbur represented two of the three individuals (with Martha Isler as the third) who were expected to provide ECI's operational leadership. Wilbur was critical both for fundraising and for maintaining ECIM's relationship with UW management; Papale had been responsible for promoting relationships with a variety of stakeholders. Wilbur was not replaced; John Sava was hired to fulfill some of the functions previously performed by Papale, but Sava's authority was not clearly defined. Later, Claire Morrison, a new vice president at UW (formerly with the state's DPW), was asked to supervise ECIM. At different times after the departure of Wilbur, ECIM reported to Sava, to Morrison, or directly to Meyer. We agree with the assessment of ECI conducted by Dickerson & Mangus, Ink., in September 1999, which identified the lack of a clearly defined chain of command as a major problem inhibiting effective administration (Dickerson & Mangus, 1999, p. 28). Although the theory of action assumed that UW and ECIM were an integrated unit (as suggested by Figure 3.1),

ECIM was never well integrated into the UW organization, so the problems with the chain of command became critical.

Another result of the departure of key staff was that individuals who had been hired to serve a specific role were given responsibilities outside their primary experience and expertise. ECIM staff were experienced in program design, but after the departure of Wilbur and Papale, ECIM was given additional responsibilities related to financial management and to relationships with both neighborhoods and funders. Some funders perceived that UW essentially discontinued the task of maintaining the support of key business leaders and contributors after Joyce Wilbur departed. More generally, UW did not hire for ECI a top executive with experience relevant to both the entrepreneurial startup of a new organization and the ongoing operation of a large-scale organization.

While key staff were departing and ECI's administrative structure was becoming more ambiguous, the number of advisory committees on the volunteer side was proliferating. The original structure included an advisory council whose function was to review community plans submitted in response to the RFNP. As chronicled in Chapter Two, UW added a preliminary review committee (PRC) in late 1997 to serve as an additional layer of review for community plans. A few months later, an ECI management committee was added to the mix, creating an additional layer of supervision on the volunteer side. The committee structure ultimately became so complex that even some of the people who served on the committees did not understand how they fit in. [6]

Consequences of Administrative Complexity

The complexity and weaknesses of ECI's leadership structure had a number of negative consequences for ECI's operation, including:

---

[6]In addition to these volunteer oversight committees, several other volunteer committees, or working groups, were established. For example, a career development committee, consisting mainly of ECE practitioners and academics, developed ECI's pre-service training curriculum. Another committee helped to establish links between ECI and Head Start programs. In our assessment, these committees had a positive influence on ECI's operation. For example, the Head Start committee laid the groundwork for ECI's collaboration with local Head Start grantees, which resulted in 20 Head Start centers becoming licensed with the state to provide full-day child care.

- *A slow process of neighborhood approvals.* The complex administrative structure and proliferation of advisory committees hampered ECI's ability to respond quickly to neighborhood plans. Community groups spent many months or even years developing proposals that met ECI standards. In some cases, ECI's various approval mechanisms—both in UW administration and the volunteer committees—took several months to either approve or fund proposals.

- *A slow response to changed conditions.* Failings of the original business plan, including the unwieldy theory of action and mistaken assumptions about supply and demand (to be discussed in Chapter Four), were apparent soon after the initiative's launch. The lack of clear leadership, however, meant that ECI's response was slow. Business plan revision did not begin until nearly two years after ECI's launch.

- *A power struggle between UW and ECIM.* Confusion over roles, especially over who had the authority to make key operational and strategic decisions, permitted disagreements between ECIM and UW management to escalate into full-blown, unresolved power struggles. UW management and ECIM developed early disagreements stemming largely from the fact that they prioritized the goals of the initiative differently. For ECIM, maintaining high-quality services was the most important goal. UW management placed a high value on serving substantial numbers of children and achieving sustainability. When costs per child turned out to be much larger than expected, ECI's goals came into tension with each other, putting ECIM and UW management at loggerheads; some of the volunteer members of ECI's complicated committee oversight structure were also involved in the struggle. The weakness of the organizational structure delayed resolution of the conflict.

The conflict between ECIM and UW management had negative consequences for ECI, both in terms of public relations and neighborhood operations. In the midst of the power struggle, communication broke down between ECI and important funders, volunteers, and business leaders, because UW management and ECIM could not agree on the message. A number of funders were left frustrated by the absence of information coming from ECI. In addition, the power struggle led to crossed signals in directions given to lead agencies. Many lead agency representatives told us of their frustration about the instability of ECI's policies, particularly in 1999 and 2000. Policy directives issued by ECIM would sometimes be rescinded by UW management the next day, according to interviewees. This kind of confusion seriously undermined confidence in ECI in the neighborhoods.

Eventually, UW management ended the power struggle in the spring of 2000 by fully asserting its authority over ECIM. Resolution occurred only after UW management confirmed that the major funders were in agreement about the need to scale ECI down. By this time, it was probably two years too late to make the major changes that might have salvaged ECI's long-term prospects.

CONCLUSION

ECI's theory of action was simultaneously bureaucratic and community based, and it exhibited the vices of both approaches and the virtues of neither. The theory of action meant that administrative costs would be substantial, that implementation would be slow, and that community control would clash with quality control. Moreover, a labyrinthine leadership structure precluded decisive response when these and other problems arose during the course of the initiative's implementation.

Chapter Four

ECI SERVICES: DEMAND, SUPPLY, AND INCENTIVES

ECI's plan to serve large numbers of children at an average cost of $4,000 to $5,000 per child was based on a number of assumptions about the demand for and supply of ECI services. Specifically, the plan made assumptions about

- The population of children who would be served

- The mix of services (e.g., full-day versus half-day, center versus family child care) that would be requested by parents and lead agencies

- The participation of existing ECE providers

Many of the assumptions made in the original business plan turned out to be far off the mark. As a result, ECI's enrollment grew much more slowly than expected and costs per child were dramatically higher.

This chapter argues that the assumptions of the original business plan were mistaken largely because insufficient attention was paid to issues related to demand, supply, and incentives. ECI's planning was complicated by its collaborative nature. ECI succeeded in bringing together a diverse group of stakeholders but did not plan for the unintended consequences that can result from collaboration. ECI's stakeholders may all have endorsed in principle the ultimate goal of long-term educational and social benefits for children and society through the provision of high-quality ECE services, but most stakeholders had other, more immediate interests as well. Parents care not only about long-term educational benefits, but also about the safety, convenience, familiarity, and hourly coverage of ECE programs. Neighborhood agencies care about community development in their neighborhoods and about their own welfare. Providers (both center and home based) care about the resources available to them and about the burdens of affiliating with ECI. And the state and its welfare department care about promoting additional public priorities, such as controlling the cost of service, providing incentives for low-income parents to work, and permitting parents to choose their children's ECE providers. Table 4.1 summarizes these interests.

In practice, the interests of parents and neighborhood agencies combined to create a demand for the most expensive variety of service contemplated in the original business plan: full-day ECE services in newly established centers. Meanwhile, the supply side of the equation looked dramatically different than expected, in part because many existing providers (especially home-based providers) perceived the costs of joining ECI as greater than the benefits.

ECI's failure to anticipate the likely desires of parents is especially striking. Although ECI's planners were strongly committed to grassroots, community-level decisionmaking, they did not fully appreciate that decisionmaking in ECE is in fact decentralized even below the community level: The most important decisionmakers are

Table 4.1

Stakeholder Interests with Respect to ECI

Stakeholder	Interests
All stakeholders	Long-term educational and social benefits for children and society
Parents	Child care that is safe, convenient, familiar, and available all day
Neighborhood agencies	Community development in the neighborhood Satisfying the desires of neighborhood parents Resources and leadership for the agency
Existing ECE providers (center and home based)	Resources for the provider Avoiding regulatory burden
State welfare department	Controlling costs Incentives for parents to work Giving parents choice of ECE providers

parents. Parental desires must be accounted for by any ECE initiative.

In this chapter, we explore how demand and supply forces diverted ECI from its original aim of providing a wide array of relatively inexpensive services with a primary emphasis on education into an umbrella for high-cost, full-day ECE programs largely delivered in new centers. We look at the potential providers of ECI services and how the business plan's incentives drove up costs and created confusion and disappointment in the neighborhoods. (Chapter Six addresses ECI's relationship with the state welfare department and other state actors.)

WHO WOULD ECI SERVE?

The ECI business plan targeted children in low-income neighborhoods who were not currently served in subsidized ECE programs. But ECI was unrealistic about its ability to exclude those who did not meet its eligibility criteria.

ECI's original business plan and its early operational implementation created considerable confusion about eligibility criteria, excluding many possible participants. The initial plan suggested that, among the children in the 80 at-risk neighborhoods, ECI would target "unserved" children—i.e., those not already in existing child-care arrangements subsidized by either the government or UW. ECIM initially tried to exclude children who were already receiving some form of registered or licensed care and to forbid eligible children from enrolling with ECI providers outside of their home neighborhoods. Although these restrictions were eventually lifted, they at first limited the number of children served and caused confusion among lead agencies and providers.

ECI's desire not to subsidize children who were not in need of its services is understandable. According to our interviewees, however, most of these "already served" children were not in high-quality programs (as defined by ECI standards) and presumably stood to benefit from ECI services. Indeed, ECI center directors and lead agency administrators heard from several parents who wanted to move their children to ECI programs because of the apparently higher-quality care offered. Politically, excluding "already served" children was untenable. This became clear quickly, and the eligibility restriction was dropped.

The inability to exclude ineligible children did not in itself undermine ECI's viability. It is possible, however, that it reduced the total social benefit of the program. ECI aimed to serve children who were most in need of high-quality ECE services. The social benefit produced from serving a child who would have received high-quality services elsewhere is lower than that produced from serving an unserved child. The targeting of services exclusively to children most in need may be impossible, particularly in community-based programs.

ECI's difficulty in targeting its services points to the fact that parental demand influences the population of children served by an ECE initiative. Demand is relevant not only to the population that will be served, but also to the kind of services demanded. The families that were actually served by ECI, whether initially "eligible" or not, were inevitably those with the greatest demand for ECE services. As we discuss next, the ECE services demanded by parents were largely full-day programs, and lead agencies sought to fulfill those demands largely in new child-care centers.

WHAT SERVICES WOULD BE REQUESTED BY PARENTS AND LEAD AGENCIES?

Service Mix and Costs

As noted in Chapter One, a key reason that ECI failed to achieve its scale and sustainability goals was that costs per child were three times as high as expected: $13,612 in 1999, compared with $4,407 expected in the original business plan. (The methods and assumptions we used for calculating these and other financial figures are described in the Appendix.) In Chapter Three, we demonstrate that an underestimation of administrative costs was partly responsible for this difference. Here we show that the specific mix of services provided under ECI also made an important (indeed, larger) contribution to the difference between expected and actual costs.

ECI's business plan encompassed a variety of different ECE services, ranging from part-day, Head Start–like enrichment and literacy programs, to full-day, center-based care and education. These different programs had widely varying price tags. The expected average cost was $4,407 per child per year (in year three of implementation), but this figure included services that were expected to range in cost from $1,728 at the low end to $8,560 for full-day, center-based care. In consequence, the mix of services provided was a critical cost driver for ECI.

Because ECI targeted unserved children, planners believed that most of the children would come from single-parent families that were receiving welfare benefits (originally AFDC, later TANF). They assumed that the children were presently unserved because their parents were not working and were caring for them at home. ECI planners thus believed that part-day services would be sufficient to meet the needs of these children and their parents. Specifically, the business plan assumed that 71 percent of participating children would enroll in part-day programs, with the remainder in full-day programs in either homes (18 percent of the total) or centers (11 percent of the total). In fact, most children who were ultimately served by ECI were in full-day, center-based care—the most expensive variety of service in the original ECI business plan. In 1999, virtually all ECI children were in full-day programs: 68 percent in new centers, 23 percent in existing centers, and 9 percent in family child-care homes.

We did a cost simulation to demonstrate the importance of the service mix to the average cost per child. Using the original business plan's estimates of the cost of each variety of service, we simulated how the shift from the projected service mix to the actual service mix would have raised the average cost per child, holding other factors constant. If ECI had correctly anticipated the distribution of services across types (e.g., part-day early literacy programs, full-day service in new centers, full-day service in existing family child-care homes), then, using its own assumptions about the cost of each particular type of service, its projected cost per child in year three (1999) would have risen from $4,407 to $7,961, an increase of 81 percent. In other words, even if ECI's *only* mistake had concerned the mix of services provided, its cost per child would have been 81 percent higher than the business plan anticipated. (Other mistaken assumptions raised costs still further, as is discussed in detail later in this chapter and in Chapter Five.) In short, *one major reason that ECI cost more per child than expected was that ECI provided more-intensive services (on average) than expected.*

The Demand for Full-Day Care

The shift from part-day programs in the business plan to full-day programs in reality caused a substantial increase in costs. Here we explore why the business plan erred about the mix of programs that would be desired by families.

ECI assumed that most of the targeted children would need only part-day services because most of the children's mothers were not working full-time outside the home. But ECI underestimated the proportion of participating children whose mothers were in the workforce. Nationally, as the economy improved between 1992 and 1996, the proportion of single women with children ages five or younger in the labor force increased from 46 percent to just under 60 percent. Employment demands often require parents, especially single parents, to find full-day care for children. The Urban Institute (Ehrle, Adams, and Tout, 2001) found that 60 percent of children ages zero to three with single parents who work are in full-day care. Another study (Smith, 2000) estimated that in 1995, children under age five with a single parent who worked or attended school spent an average of 35 hours per week in nonparental child care (see also Hofferth et al., 1998). Interview respondents familiar with local Head Start programs pointed out that in the early and mid-1990s, program staff noticed that many eligible parents were not enrolling their children because the half-day program schedule conflicted with parents' full-day work schedules. This problem was evident in Head Start centers across the nation (Besharov, 1996; Zigler and Muenchow, 1992).

With welfare reform, the demand for full-day care grew. Welfare reform accelerated the trend of putting mothers into the paid labor force: By 1998 (the latest year for which data are available), the proportion of single mothers with children under six who were working had climbed to 67 percent (Blau, 2001). In Pennsylvania, the number of families receiving TANF (formerly AFDC) dropped by 50 percent between 1994 and 1999 as women moved into the workforce (Committee on Ways and Means, 2000, Table 7-5). A recent study of mothers making the transition from welfare found that many mothers with part-time jobs relied on full-day care. The researchers speculate that this was due to mothers' difficulty in matching their work schedules with child-care schedules (Fuller and Kagan, 2000).

Welfare reform should not have come as a surprise, however. Pennsylvania's welfare-reform legislation passed in mid-1996, at the end of the ECI planning period but a month prior to the approval of the business plan by the UW board. Indeed, several ECI planners told us that during the planning phase (from late 1994 until UW approval of ECI implementation in June 1996), they knew that welfare reform was coming, although they were uncertain of what the implications would be for recipients' child-care needs. The plan did not include any analysis of how sensitive its projections were to this uncertainty.

In summary, welfare reform contributed to the higher-than-expected demand for full-day services, but it should not have come as a complete surprise. Moreover, it was not the only or perhaps even the primary reason that the business plan's projected service mix was so far off. There is good evidence that many parents wanted full-day care even prior to welfare reform. And parents who had the greatest need for child care were probably the ones who were most likely to seek out ECI's services. Moreover, a parental preference for full-day care is unsurprising if parents are given a choice of full- or part-day care and both options are largely or entirely subsidized. Large numbers of parents—whether low- or high-income, employed or not— are likely to prefer more hours of child care and education if it is offered at little or no additional cost. This is essentially the choice that ECI offered.[1]

Incentives to Neighborhood Agencies

The reaction of neighborhood leaders to the choice offered by ECI should have been as predictable as the reaction of parents. ECI's promise to neighborhoods that they could "dream big" gave the communities every reason to ask for the best, most-expensive services on the menu. Such services were consistent with the desires of the parents who were the lead agencies' constituents, and were also likely to promote the largest amount of development in the neighborhoods and greatest benefits for the agencies themselves, particu-

---

[1]ECI did charge parents weekly fees that were somewhat higher for full-day care than for part-day care. But even these higher fees were minimal (ranging from $5 to $30 per week for a family of three with an annual income at or below the poverty level). For many children, ECI paid 90 percent or more of the total cost of care.

larly if they included major capital investments for new child-care centers. This point is not a criticism of the lead agencies or other neighborhood leaders. Their mission is to serve their neighborhoods, their constituents, and the interests of their agencies. It was entirely reasonable for them to attempt to bring the largest amount of resources possible into their neighborhoods and agencies. But ECI's planners should have expected this when they gave the neighborhoods a menu of options from which to choose, especially given that ECI actively encouraged the neighborhood groups to plan ambitiously.

This effect was apparent not only in the shift from part-day to full-day programs, but also in neighborhood requests for capital funding. ECI approved an expensive, high-profile capital investment for a new child-care center in one of the early neighborhood plans. Not surprisingly, many other neighborhood planning groups also wanted major infrastructure investments. It soon became clear, however, that ECI could not afford the same level of investment in every community. Realizing that the cost of building and renovating new centers was greater than anticipated, ECIM (under pressure from UW management) began to restrict the amount of funds provided for capital projects.

More generally, ECI funds were invested in a variety of ways, and it is not obvious that investment decisions were made with a clear sense of strategic priorities. ECI was inconsistent in what it agreed to fund from one community to the next, partly as a result of disagreements between ECIM and UW, and partly as a result of growing recognition about the need for cost control. Funding decisions were typically based on individual negotiations with each lead agency, but inconsistencies across neighborhoods left some lead agencies disappointed that their "big dreams" could not be realized.

The incentives that ECI created for neighborhood agencies were problematic not only in the planning process, but also in operations. Until the last few months of ECI's existence at UW, funding was provided to lead agencies and providers on a line item basis, rather than a per-child capitated rate. Although an initial infusion of funds was necessary to begin lead agency operations when new providers were being created, the continued use of line item funding had two unfortunate effects. First, it meant that ECIM had to closely scrutinize lead agency budgeting, creating a substantial administrative burden for ECIM and increasing friction with the lead agencies. Second, it meant that lead agencies had little incentive to find ways to reduce costs. This was true in lead agency interactions with contracted ECE providers as well: In their relations with contracted providers, lead agencies were simply passing along funds provided by ECI, and they therefore had little reason to drive hard bargains with providers whose success they hoped to promote.

ECI might have avoided these problems, and thereby reduced costs, if it had had an investment plan that sent clear signals and appropriate incentives to lead agencies and providers. Two other directions might have been considered. One possibility would have given more real discretion to the neighborhood agencies to design their programs while placing clear limits on the amount of funding that would be provided. Alternatively, ECI might have defined the service options more narrowly and more explicitly.

Unfortunately, ECI's original business plan did not provide a compelling explanation for offering a wide variety of service options at a wide variety of costs. The plan argued that high-quality ECE services would produce long-term cost-benefit advantages and simply assumed that the $2,000 services received by some children would be equivalent to the $9,000 services received by others. Parents and neighborhood agencies, however, recognized that the services were in fact quite different; not surprisingly, they chose the highest-intensity, most-expensive services.

WHO WOULD PROVIDE ECI SERVICES?

The surest way to enroll large numbers of children rapidly is to go where they are, making maximum use of existing ECE providers. Although the business plan expected that many existing providers would become ECI providers, in practice many were left out. Existing providers did not participate in ECI for three reasons:

- ECIM believed that many existing providers operated at so low a level of quality that they were incapable of providing high-quality services.

- Some community planning groups chose to exclude existing providers.

- Some existing providers chose not to participate because they considered the quality standards and monitoring process too intrusive.

In short, the goal of serving large numbers of children was in tension with both ECI's quality standards and enforcement and its desire to promote community control.

Both providers and community representatives (e.g., lead agency directors and administrators) told us that ECIM discouraged them from including some existing providers in their plans. As a result of early inspections, ECIM concluded that quality in some established child-care centers was so low that it would be better to establish new, high-quality child-care centers. In some instances, initial inspections by ECIM uncovered substantial violations of state licensing requirements. Rather than work with these providers to improve, ECIM encouraged community groups to focus on creating new programs.

Meanwhile, many lead agency directors were happy to start new ECE services. Simply increasing capacity was an important goal in some neighborhoods (as in Braddock, for example, which lacked center-based care of any kind). And the creation of new centers gave a number of lead agencies the opportunity to expand the scope and reach of the services provided by their agencies. Moreover, many had doubts of their own about the quality of existing centers in their neighborhoods.

The judgment of ECIM and some community planning groups that existing providers could not provide high-quality care may have been correct.[2] But even if new providers under the supervision of ECIM and lead agencies could provide higher-quality care than existing providers could, bypassing the existing providers dramatically reduced ECI's ability to reach large numbers of children quickly. It may also have raised the capital costs of the initiative.

---

[2]Because an assessment of service quality was not within the scope of our study, we make no judgment on this issue one way or the other.

New Providers and Capital Costs

ECI's focus on creating new providers meant that physical facilities needed to be found. Unfortunately, many of the neighborhoods lacked adequate, code-ready space. In the first three years of implementation (the only years for which we have complete data), capital expenditures accounted for about 24 percent of the total spent, substantially above the 17 percent that had been budgeted for the first three years in the original business plan. Amortized capital costs amounted to $697 per child in 1999, compared to $155 per child in the original plan.

Nearly all of the difference between planned and actual capital costs is explained by the shift to full-day, center-based services. A simulated model, showing ECI's estimated costs using the actual service mix and the business plan's estimates of the cost of each kind of service, shows that capital costs would have been predicted to reach $642 per child. (Again, details can be found in the Appendix.) That is, it appears that ECI's planners did not dramatically underestimate the capital cost associated with opening new centers. The capital cost per child was higher than expected largely because a high proportion of children were in new centers. Greater use of existing centers might have reduced the total capital cost.

New Providers, Line Item Funding, and Fixed Operating Costs

Extensive reliance on new centers also meant that ECI had to endure the high costs of the startup period, when center staff had to be employed but enrollment was relatively low. More generally, ECI's original business plan made the mistake of assuming that children in centers that were less than fully enrolled could be served for the same cost per child as those in fully enrolled centers.

The business plan assumed that, within a particular class of service, the cost of serving the first child enrolled in a center was the same as the cost of serving the last child enrolled. In other words, the plan assumed that all operating costs of a center were variable rather than fixed.[3] Such an assumption might be reasonable for pre-existing centers, where, rather than providing line item funding for all operational costs, ECI intended to provide a capitated reimbursement amount for each ECI child served. It would also be reasonable for family child-care homes, which hire no employees and which were given the same amount of funding for each child.

In fact, however, the great majority of ECI children were served in newly established centers. Capitated funding would have been unworkable for new centers, which need to hire staff prior to enrolling their first children. Indeed, according to several lead agency administrators and providers whom we interviewed, ECIM required them to hire a full staff of caregivers before a single child was enrolled. Recognizing that this required up-front funding, ECI provided line item funding for salaries and other operational expenses in new centers. According to our interviewees, salaries and benefits constituted the overwhelming majority of operational expenses. But this meant that, in practice, the operating costs of the centers were largely fixed, regardless of the number of children served. In consequence, the cost per child was not the same for all children: the lower the number of children enrolled in a program, the higher the cost per child.

Indeed, fixed costs are a problem not only for newly opened centers, but for all centers that operate at less than 100 percent of capacity. Providers cannot prorate the pay of their employees based on the number of children served. If a classroom is a few children short of capacity, a center still has to pay a teacher. ECI's staff-to-child ratio and maximum group size requirements further constrained programs' ability to vary operating requirements according to the number of children enrolled.

Lacking direct experience in the business of ECE, ECI's pro bono consultants who assisted in the development of the business plan did not recognize that child-care center costs are largely fixed. The business plan recognized that enrollment in new centers would grow gradually over time, but it mistakenly assumed that cost per child was independent of enrollment. The plan's estimates of cost per

---

[3]By contrast, the business plan recognized that capital costs were fixed for each center.

child were built on models of fully enrolled centers, but actual cost per child in centers that were less than fully enrolled was necessarily higher. In the real world, most centers do not operate at 100 percent of capacity. When ECI centers opened, enrollments grew gradually over time and in most cases never reached 100 percent of capacity. (In 1999, average enrollment at ECI centers over the course of the year was 72.6 percent of capacity; this figure was increasing over the course of the year.) As a result, operating cost per child was higher than projected in the original business plan. The fault here lies not with the lead agencies or the providers, but with the variable-cost assumption of the original business plan, which was not realistic. In Chapter Five, we estimate the magnitude of the effect of this assumption on ECI's costs.

ECI and Family Child-Care Providers

A final reason that ECI relied largely on new providers was that some existing providers opted not to participate. According to our interviewees, some existing child-care centers perceived that the burdens of conforming to ECI quality standards, submitting to regular inspections, and adhering to requirements for staff qualifications and compensation were not worth the rewards of participating in ECI. While this was a problem for enrolling child-care centers, it was even more of an obstacle to enrolling family child-care providers.

ECI's original business plan assumed that, among children in full-day programs, more would be enrolled in family child-care than in centers. ECI's desire to include family child-care providers was based on an accurate understanding that they constitute a large part of the child-care market in low-income neighborhoods. Evidence suggests that a large proportion of parents with low incomes or little education prefer informal forms of care, such as relatives' and neighbors' family child-care homes, many of which are unregistered. Anderson and Levine (1999, p. 9) found that "children of less-skilled mothers are more than twice as likely to be cared for by a relative than children of the most-skilled mothers." Similar conclusions were reached in a recent study by researchers at the Urban Institute (Ehrle, Adams, and Tout, 2001). Recognizing this, ECI hoped to enroll a substantial number of family child-care homes. ECI's planners anticipated that 132 family child-care providers would serve 528 ECI children in 1999.

Several community planning groups attempted to recruit unregulated family child-care homes. But getting these providers to attend meetings or express an interest in ECI was difficult. According to several of our interviewees, some unregulated providers initially considered becoming ECI providers but lost interest once they learned that they would be subject to regular home inspections and observations by quality assurance monitors. The first step toward becoming an ECI provider involved registration with the state, which many family providers apparently wanted to avoid. It is widely believed that many unregulated providers do not report their income to tax authorities, which they would have to do if they became registered.

To participate in ECI, family child-care providers were required to complete a 50-hour pre-service training course and to obtain 24 hours of additional training each year. As a family child-care provider, simply finding the time to complete the training requirements would be a challenge. Some family child-care providers (or residents interested in becoming family child-care providers) started ECI's pre-service training program but dropped out before completing it. Others completed their training but dropped out during the next phase of the process, when ECI staff would have inspected their homes and developed a plan for needed improvements. Still others dropped out after ECI had purchased equipment, curriculum materials, or home improvements for them.

The result of ECI's efforts to enroll family child-care providers is not encouraging. As of August 2000 (a month after the full initiative formally ended), 128 individuals had participated in ECI's pre-service training for family child-care providers; 99 had completed the training; 45 had registered with the state; and only 24 were actively participating in ECI, serving just 68 children.[4]

---

[4]Some who completed the family child-care pre-service training ended up being hired by ECI centers to fill direct caregiving staff positions. Nonetheless, the majority of those trained did not stay with ECI in any capacity. Many of the community representatives that we interviewed believe that most of these individuals are caring for children in their homes. It is possible that, because of their ECI training, they are providing a higher quality of care than they would have otherwise.

ECI's inability to enroll substantial numbers of family child-care providers inevitably reduced its reach. While ECIM did not assume that high-quality services had to be delivered in centers, the great majority of its capacity was in fact center based. Many parents, however, strongly prefer that care be provided either by someone the child and family already know and trust (e.g., a relative or neighbor) or in an environment similar to the child's own home, as opposed to a structured, center-based environment with highly trained caregivers (Brown-Lyons, Robertson, and Layzer, 2001). Indeed, for many parents, "quality" care may be defined in terms of the familiarity and intimacy of a family child-care environment. The new centers that were offered by ECI may not have appealed to parents who were content with existing family-care arrangements.

In fairness to ECI, we know of no program that has solved the problem of getting substantial numbers of unregulated family child-care providers to join a high-quality, regulated system. Many ECE initiatives simply ignore family child care entirely. Although ECI did not solve the problem, its plan at least recognized that family child care is in fact an important component of the ECE market. Unfortunately, it did not recognize the extent to which family child-care providers would be deterred by the perceived barriers and costs of participating in ECI.

The Supply of Qualified Labor

Several lead agencies and providers had difficulty finding and retaining center and classroom staff that met ECI's minimum qualification standards.[5] Nearly all community stakeholders we interviewed spoke of this problem, which was a challenge with respect to both center staff and lead agency quality monitors (who were expected to have a master's degree in early childhood or child development). Even though compensation for staff in ECI centers was higher than that of typical child-care and early-education workers, ECI centers still had difficulty competing with school districts for qualified staff. In September 1999, teaching staff at several ECI centers left for

---

[5]Family child-care providers were exempt from ECI's minimum staff qualification requirements. ECIM recognized that most of these providers would have little formal education beyond high school.

teaching positions at area schools. In some centers, positions went unfilled for long periods. To a certain extent, this problem was heightened by ECIM's requirement that lead agencies and providers look first to the local community for staff. Over the course of the initiative, lead agencies and providers found it increasingly difficult to find local applicants who met ECI's minimum education requirements. ECI's compensation standards also created problems for some lead agencies, which found themselves in the awkward position of having to provide a benefit package to their ECI staff while not doing so for staff in non-ECI programs.

CONCLUSION

ECI was undermined by demand and supply forces that dramatically changed the course of the initiative. In particular, the children served, the services provided, and the service providers differed substantially from what the original business plan had expected. Most notably, ECI shifted from an intended focus on low-cost, part-day preschool services to an actual service menu dominated by high-cost, full-day child-care centers. The changes in the service menu and other problems related to demand, supply, and incentives were at least partly attributable to oversights and flawed assumptions in ECI's original business plan. The following chapter explores how those oversights and flawed assumptions affected ECI's costs.

Chapter Five

EXPLAINING ECI'S COSTS

Chapters Three and Four describe several reasons for the mismatch between ECI's expected and actual costs per child. These include underestimates of administrative and capital costs, a change in the service mix to full-day, center-based services, and a failure to account for the fact that per-child costs are higher at centers that are not fully enrolled (i.e., most operational costs at centers are largely fixed). Here we return to the cost issue to examine the relative magnitudes of different reasons for the underestimation of costs.

We examine the issue in several ways. First, we separate planned and actual costs into central administration, capital, and neighborhood/operating costs, showing the proportional difference in each category. Next, we examine how the picture changes when costs are examined in terms of child-hours of service rather than child-years of service. The bulk of the chapter then examines the results of two simulations that estimate what ECI's expected costs would have been if two key assumptions of the business plan—related to the service mix and the fixed costs of new centers—had accurately reflected the ultimate reality.

EXPECTED AND ACTUAL COSTS BY COMPONENT

Consider the proportional difference between actual and expected costs for the categories of central administration, capital, and neighborhood/operating costs. Total cost per child in 1999 ($13,612) was 3.1 times as high as expected cost ($4,407). Table 5.1 shows the proportional and dollar increases for these three components of total costs.

81

Table 5.1

Difference Between Expected and Actual Costs, 1999

Component	Expected Cost per Child	Actual Cost per Child	Difference	Multiplier
Central administration	286	1,231	946	4.3
Capital	155	697	542	4.5
Neighborhood/operating	3,966	11,684	7,717	2.9
Total	4,407	13,612	9,205	3.1

By this measure, all categories of expenses were dramatically higher than expected. This table does not consider the effect of the service mix, however, which had major implications for both capital and neighborhood/operating costs.

COST PER CHILD-HOUR

As noted in Chapter Four, the change in the service mix was one prominent reason that costs were higher than expected. ECI was providing more hours of service per child than planned, because virtually all children in the program were in full-day services rather than in the part-day services the business plan had expected to predominate. Neighborhood agency representatives understood this point quite well. In our interviews, they argued that cost comparisons should account for the greater number of hours of service being provided to each child. According to our interviewees, the typical child was in fact in service for 10 hours per day. When considered on an *hourly* basis, implicitly adjusting for the intensity of the services, ECI's expected cost of $3.02 per child-hour compares to an actual cost of $5.24 per child-hour.[1] While the difference between expected and actual cost per child-hour is much smaller proportionally than the difference between expected and actual cost per child-year, it remains substantial.

Whether annual or hourly cost is the more appropriate measure depends on the comparative net social benefits of part-day versus full-

---

[1]If the average length of service was less than 10 hours daily, true cost would be somewhat higher than $5.24.

day ECE programs. Unfortunately, no research exists to answer this question definitively. In terms of *care*, presumably a full-day program (notionally 10 hours) produces about three times the benefit of a part-day program (notionally 3.5 hours), and cost per hour is the appropriate measure. But in terms of *education*, it is not clear that the benefit scales linearly with the number of contact hours. For example, a three-year-old child may derive a substantial educational benefit from three hours of education daily, but hours four through 10 may provide only a small additional educational benefit. However, it is also possible that a substantial educational benefit is realized only above a threshold number of hours per service. None of the existing research on the benefits of high-quality ECE can answer these questions and identify the marginal benefit of additional hours of care. It should be noted, however, that Perry Preschool, the most frequently cited example of a high-quality ECE program with demonstrated long-term benefits, operated on a part-day basis.

When ECI was launched, its business plan focused on the number of children to be served, not the number of hours of service to be provided. Our interviews confirm that most of ECI's stakeholders saw ECI's goal as serving a large number of children, independent of the number of hours of service. For those stakeholders and in ECI's own terms, cost per child-year is likely to be a better measure than cost per child-hour. We therefore focused most of our analysis on the cost per child-year. Nevertheless, we believe that it is important to account for the service mix as a key explanation for ECI's costs, and our adjustment for the service mix implicitly accounts for the increased number of hours of service provided.

ADJUSTING FOR SERVICE MIX

As noted in Chapter Four, the shift from 71 percent part-time service (in the plan) to 100 percent full-time (and largely center-based) programs (in actuality) would have driven the cost per child up from $4,407 to $7,961 even if all the business plan's assumptions about the costs of specific kinds of care had been correct. Figure 5.1 breaks out the costs of capital, central administration, and neighborhood-level operating expenses. The first bar in the figure describes costs projected in the original business plan; the third bar shows costs actually incurred by ECI. The second bar illustrates the simulated result based on the original business plan's assumptions with respect to component costs: Administrative cost per child is independent of service mix, but operating and capital costs vary for different kinds of services. If ECI had correctly estimated the actual service mix in advance, its own assumptions about the costs of specific services would have led to the predicted costs shown in the second bar of Figure 5.1, for a total of $7,961, not $4,407. (Detailed tables can be found in the Appendix.)

More specifically, the change in service mix by itself would have raised capital costs from $155 to $642 per child and neighborhood/operating costs from $3,966 to $7,033 per child. In sum, the service mix explains nearly all of the increase in capital costs and a substantial part of the increase in operating costs. The difference between the simulated result of $7,961 and the actual cost of $13,612 must be explained by factors other than the service mix.

ADJUSTING FOR FIXED COSTS

In addition to its mistaken assumption about service mix, the cost analysis in the original plan contained the erroneous assumption

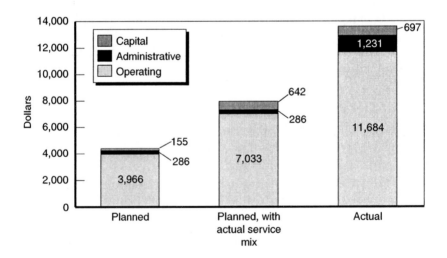

Figure 5.1—Effect of Service Mix on Cost per Child-Year, 1999

that all operating costs at centers would be completely variable. As a result, the operating cost per child served by a center was projected to be the same (what it would be at full enrollment) regardless of the number of children enrolled. In reality, ECI centers' operating costs were mostly fixed, as we describe in Chapter Four: Staff had to be hired before opening, and salaries had to be paid even if a center was not filled to capacity. Moreover, requirements about group sizes and staff-to-child ratios further constrained providers' ability to vary their operating costs with enrollment. If the business plan had recognized that the operating costs of centers were largely fixed, it would have predicted a much more conservative (i.e., higher) estimate of the cost per child, especially during the scale-up period, when new centers were opening and their enrollments were increasing gradually.

We can estimate the magnitude of the effect of less-than-100-percent enrollment on the cost per child-year by adjusting initial estimates of cost with a factor that accounts for actual enrollment rates. This estimate is subject to some uncertainty because the data were incomplete and a number of assumptions were required.[2] Moreover, the adjustment is likely to be somewhat inflated because it assumes that all costs in child-care centers are fixed despite the fact that some costs are likely to vary with enrollment. For example, centers that are less than fully enrolled will use fewer disposable supplies (e.g., crayons and books) than will fully enrolled centers. We believe that these variable costs are likely to be relatively small. Nevertheless, it should be recognized that this adjustment produces an upper-bound estimate of the cost per child. (From a business planning perspective, such an adjustment might be considered prudently conservative.)

We estimate that ECI centers were enrolled at an average rate of 72.6 percent of capacity in 1999 (with the enrollment rate gradually increasing over the course of the year). If ECI's planners had assumed that operating costs in centers were fixed (and if they had accurately estimated a 72.6 percent enrollment rate in 1999), they would have inflated their estimates of the per-child operating cost of center-based service by dividing by 0.726.

---

[2]In particular, data were incomplete with respect to both ECI capacity and enrollment. The data limitations and the assumptions made to surmount them are described in the Appendix.

Figure 5.2 adds a new bar to Figure 5.1 to show the results of applying this adjustment to the previous adjustment for the service mix. As can be seen, if the business plan had both anticipated the actual service mix and accounted for fixed operating costs in centers, it would have predicted ECI's cost per child to be as high as $10,373 (including $9,445 in neighborhood/operating cost) rather than the $4,407 actually predicted. To reiterate, the estimate of $10,373 is probably somewhat high because it assumes that all center-based operating costs are fixed even though centers can in fact probably save a limited amount of money when enrollment is below capacity. It should be considered an upper-bound figure that provides a rough estimate of the additional costs that are explained by the predictable fixed costs of operating child-care centers.

SUMMARY OF COST FACTORS

With the aid of the simulations that adjust for both service mix and fixed operating costs in child-care centers, we can re-examine the relative differences between simulated and actual costs for adminis-

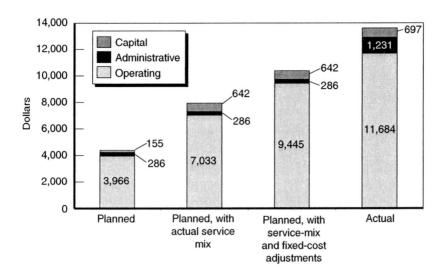

Figure 5.2—Effect of Service Mix and Fixed Costs on Cost per Child-Year, 1999

trative, capital, and neighborhood/operating expenses. Table 5.2 replicates Table 5.1, except that a column showing the simulated cost with the service-mix and fixed-cost corrections replaces the estimated costs from the original business plan. Table 5.2 thus compares the actual cost in each category of expenditure with the cost *that would have been expected had the original business plan accounted for the actual service mix and the fixed operating costs of child-care centers.*

The simulations do not affect the results for administrative costs, which should be largely unaffected by service mix and entirely unaffected by the fixed-cost adjustment to center-based operating costs. As noted previously, the service mix adjustment dramatically increased simulated capital costs; as a result, actual capital costs were only 9 percent higher than simulated capital costs. Both adjustments raise expected neighborhood/operating costs substantially. Actual neighborhood/operating costs remain higher than the simulated prediction, but only by 24 percent. Total cost per child exceeds the simulated cost by 31 percent, which is dramatically less than the 211 percent by which total cost exceeds the business plan's original estimate. These results strongly suggest that the business plan's flawed assumptions about service mix and fixed costs account for a large proportion of ECI's cost overrun.

We can estimate the relative significance of the service-mix and fixed-cost adjustments alongside remaining capital, administrative, and neighborhood/operating costs in explaining the total difference between ECI's planned ($4,407) and actual ($13,612) cost per child.

Table 5.2

Difference Between Simulated and Actual Costs, 1999

Component	Simulated Cost per Child with Service-Mix and Fixed-Cost Adjustments	Actual Cost per Child	Difference	Multiplier
Central administration	286	1,231	946	4.30
Capital	642	697	55	1.09
Neighborhood/operating	9,445	11,684	2,238	1.24
Total	10,373	13,612	3,239	1.31

In total, the difference between estimated and actual cost per child is $13,612 minus $4,407, or $9,205. The mistaken assumptions about service mix and variable costs together explain as much as 65 percent of this difference.[3] It is not possible to cleanly separate the effects of these two assumptions, however, because they interact with each other. We therefore lump them together here as "business plan assumptions that proved false." As in the preceding analysis, this represents an upper-bound estimate because some center-based operating costs may be variable rather than fixed. Figure 5.3 shows how central administrative costs and additional operating and capital costs (not already explained by the service mix) compare to the flawed business plan assumptions in explaining the total difference between planned and expected cost per child.

The importance of capital costs is explained almost entirely by the service mix. Capital costs were substantially higher than expected in total, but this was largely because a higher proportion of children than expected were served in new child-care centers. Additional capital costs, beyond those predicted by the service mix, explain less than 1 percent of the difference between actual and expected costs.

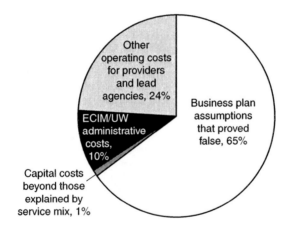

Figure 5.3—Factors Explaining the Difference Between Planned and Actual Cost per Child-Year, 1999

---

[3]The difference between $10,373 (simulated) and $4,407 (actual) is $5,966, which is 65 percent of the total difference, $9,205.

Administrative costs were far higher than expected. Nevertheless, their magnitude is small when compared to the combined effect of the service-mix and fixed-cost corrections. Administrative costs explain 10 percent of the total difference between actual and planned cost per child. As we argue in Chapter Three, however, ECI's theory of action required substantial administrative costs, probably far in excess of those that were budgeted. Arguably, then, the excess administrative cost could be added to the "business plan assumptions that proved false."

After we account for underestimates related to service mix, fixed operating costs, capital costs, and central administrative costs of ECIM and UW, the remaining neighborhood-level costs for lead agencies and service provision explain perhaps 24 percent of the difference between expected and actual cost per child (which may be a slight underestimate if the fixed cost adjustment is overestimated).

Unfortunately, we do not have sufficient data to break the neighborhood/operating costs down further. It is likely that some of these were additional administrative costs incurred by lead agencies as they hired the supervisory staff required by ECI. We have no indication that lead agencies were wasteful in their use of resources, but ECI's theory of action required the creation of an administrative structure at the lead agency level as well as at the central level. It seems likely that the business plan underestimated this expense as well as the central administrative expense. The costs of lead agency administrative staff were likely to be especially important when many lead agencies enrolled relatively small numbers of children.

CONCLUSION

The interpretation of ECI's total cost of $13,612 per child depends to a great extent on the frame of reference. Compared to the budgeted amount of $4,407, it seems astonishingly high. But it is important to remember that high-quality, full-day ECE programs generally cost substantially more than $4,407. Two of Pittsburgh's most prominent full-day ECE programs, each of which has a strong reputation for quality, range in cost from $8,500 to $9,200 per child per year (including operating and capital costs). Moreover, these programs do not need to incur quality monitoring costs; they have no central administration or lead agency to support. Minus the cost of central administration, ECI's costs amounted to $11,916, which still includes lead agency administrative costs. If all administrative costs could be separately accounted for, ECI's cost of actual service delivery might be comparable to that of other high-quality, full-day ECE programs.

Nevertheless, it is clear that ECI's business plan and operation ensured that costs would be dramatically higher than expected. The theory of action virtually guaranteed that administrative costs would be high. In addition, planners failed to anticipate the predictable demands of parents and lead agencies, which moved the initiative toward providing the more-costly, full-time, center-based care. Indeed, ECI ultimately looked quite different than many of its original advocates and funders had intended. And the difference between planned and actual cost had important implications for ECI's long-term viability, a topic to which we turn in the next chapter.

Chapter Six

SUSTAINABILITY AND THE STRATEGY TO SECURE STATE FUNDING

ECI's goal of sustainability was predicated on securing public funding from the state of Pennsylvania. ECI was expected to cost $26 million per year when it reached full scale, and its planners knew that it could not be sustained permanently with private funding. The original business plan therefore called for a focused effort, over the course of the first three years of program implementation, to persuade the state to take over the major responsibility for funding the program after five years of operation. ECI's planners had some reason for optimism, because many states were beginning to increase their investments in ECE as a result of growing awareness of its potential long-term benefits. Moreover, planners hoped to take advantage of personal and political connections between business leaders who supported ECI and the governor. Later, when it became clear that a direct commitment of state funding devoted specifically to ECI was not forthcoming, a revised business plan sought to make ECI sustainable by tapping existing state funding streams, primarily those consisting of child-care subsidies for low-income parents.

ECI's planners recognized that persuading the state to commit public funds to ECI would be a challenge, but they may have underestimated how difficult it would be. Some of the obstacles to securing state funding were substantial, and ECI made the task more difficult than it might have been. The bulk of this chapter examines the problems that undermined both ECI's initial state funding strategy and its redirected effort to achieve sustainability using the state subsidy system.

CHALLENGES FOR THE STATE STRATEGY

Diffuse Benefits and Concentrated Costs

A working assumption of the ECI plan was that ECI represented such an outstanding societal investment that the relevant stakeholders would embrace it. A strong societal benefit/cost ratio, however, is not necessarily sufficient to ensure universal support, because even programs that help society as a whole can hurt particular constituencies or, less dramatically, simply not offer them compelling advantages.

In the case of ECI, this disjunction between parochial and societal interest helps to explain why the state government did not seize the opportunity to take up the investment. Consider the breakdown of the $7 societal savings per dollar invested that was projected based on the Perry Preschool evaluation (Schweinhart, Barnes, and Weikart, 1993). First of all, benefits were expected to accrue to multiple levels of government. While ECI wanted the state to pay the bill, some of the benefits would accrue to local government (e.g., reduced costs of educational services), and some would accrue to the federal government (e.g., most of the additional tax collections expected to result). Second, the state benefits would come to various departments, but it would be difficult to spread the cost among departments because bureaucracies are stove-piped: Each department is largely independent, and funds cannot be easily transferred across departments. In practice, ECI's lobbying effort focused on Pennsylvania's Department of Public Welfare (DPW). But if DPW wanted to invest in ECI, it could not have "billed" the state corrections system (for which larger savings were expected) in anticipation of future savings. And who wins and loses in legislative appropriations is part of a much larger political dance. (See Schorr, 1989, for a discussion of these problems.)

Third, the largest component of societal benefits does not accrue to government at all. The majority of the projected societal savings ($4.66 per dollar invested) would come as reduced costs to people who, in the absence of high-quality ECE, would later be victimized by crime (Schweinhart, Barnes, and Weikart, 1993). Such savings are real and important, but they do not translate directly into revenue streams for state government.

In summary, a high societal benefit/cost ratio is compelling to the mythical social planner or benevolent dictator, but may or may not be similarly compelling to actual government decisionmakers.

Short Time Horizons

The disjunction between societal and parochial benefits can be particularly poignant for elected officials whose time horizons do not extend beyond the next election. When the majority of the benefits created by an intervention targeted at three- or four-year-olds stem from preventing crimes they would otherwise later commit, it is clear that those benefits will not be generated for at least a decade. In contrast, program costs are incurred up front. Even many of the educational benefits of such an intervention will not be seen in the first three years of its operation, when the state commitment must be made. The societal benefit-cost analysis in Schweinhart, Barnes, and Weikart, 1993, discounts costs and benefits back to the present at a rate that reflects society's overall discount rate (in this case, 3 percent annually), but an individual political leader might apply a higher rate and hence be less convinced that the program will pay off soon enough to serve his or her private interest.

Regional Politics in Pennsylvania

The amount of funding that planners hoped the state would contribute to ECI—most of the $26 million annual cost when the program reached countywide scale—was large enough to inevitably raise issues of regional fairness among Pennsylvania political leaders. As a number of our interviewees pointed out, the only way that the governor and state legislature would be able to consider providing resources on that scale to Allegheny County would be if comparable resources were provided for other parts of the state. This meant not only that complicated negotiations in the legislature would be needed, but also that the total price tag to the state would be dramatically higher. Some ECI planners hoped that state policymakers would be impressed enough with ECI's short-term results that they would want to fund similar initiatives throughout the state, using ECI as a model. On other issues, regional "logrolling" has been successful in inducing the state to provide large amounts of public funding for regional projects (most notably, for new football and baseball stadiums for both Pittsburgh and Philadelphia). Given historic attitudes in Pennsylvania toward state involvement in child care, however, ECI was to prove a difficult sell, as we describe below.

Doubtful Public Commitment to ECE

Across the country, voters and policymakers show considerable ambivalence about public funding of ECE. Some feel strongly that young children should be at home with a parent. This group also tends to believe that the responsibility for preventing children from failing in school or becoming pregnant as a teenager, involved in crime, or dependent on welfare lies with parents, not with social programs. Thus, these voters and policymakers are not persuaded by arguments that link publicly subsidized ECE programs with alleviation of these social problems (Schorr, 1989).

Nevertheless, ECI's planners had reason to believe that attitudes about public support for ECE were becoming more favorable across the country. Increasing attention to brain research demonstrating the importance of early childhood mental development was leading a number of states to increase their investment in ECE. Some states, such as California, New Jersey, and Texas, now have large-scale state-funded preschool programs that each serve over 100,000 children.

State-level interest and leadership clearly make a difference to the prospects for public funding of ECE. In Pennsylvania, ECI leaders faced a state government that has a history of conservatism when it comes to funding ECE programs (relative to other states). Although Pennsylvania has in recent years increased the resources it devotes to ECE (primarily through its child-care subsidy programs), it trails many other states in its financial commitment to ECE. For example, Pennsylvania is one of only seven states that do not fund any prekindergarten programs (National Center for Children in Poverty, 2000).[1] Pennsylvania is also one of 29 states that do not provide supplemental funding to Head Start programs (which receive funds

---

[1]Pennsylvania does permit school districts to spend some state funds designated for K–12 programs on prekindergarten programs for four year olds, but few school districts choose to do so (National Center for Children in Poverty, 2000).

directly from the federal government) (Education Week, 2002). While Pennsylvania has transferred funds from its federal Temporary Assistance for Needy Families (TANF) grant to child-care subsidies, it has done so at a rate well below the national average.[2] Moreover, the state's DPW has generally viewed its involvement in ECE as focusing on care rather than education: Promoting quality takes a back seat to the more basic task of providing child-care subsidies that will permit low-income mothers to go to work. In the mid-1990s, Pennsylvania's Department of Education (and the governor's policy office, which had considerable influence in education issues) showed little interest in ECE, instead focusing on K–12 schooling. In light of these facts, any commitment to devote substantial funding to high-quality ECE programs would involve a major departure from the state's historical attitude toward public funding of ECE.[3]

PROBLEMS WITH ECI'S STATE STRATEGY

Although the inherent obstacles to securing state funding were substantial, and Pennsylvania's policy context was especially unfriendly to public funding for ECE, ECI also made the task more difficult on its own. The first problem was one of tactics and process: ECI's engagement with state policymakers was less effective than it might have been. The second, and deeper problem, was an unacknowledged conflict with the state's welfare-reform priorities. As Table 4.1 indicates (see Chapter Four), the state of Pennsylvania has a number of goals that may be in some tension with ECI's overall goal of pro-

---

[2]In fiscal year 2000, Pennsylvania transferred only 9 percent of its TANF grant to its Child Care and Development Fund (CCDF) budget (which funds the subsidy program for former welfare families and working-poor families), compared to a national average transfer of 14 percent and a maximum transfer permitted by the federal government of 30 percent. Moreover, Pennsylvania allocated only 1 percent ($13.9 million) of its TANF grant directly to child-care subsidies for TANF recipients in work or training programs, compared to a national average of 6 percent (Education Week, 2002).

[3]As of this year (2002), state policymakers in Pennsylvania have begun giving some additional attention to issues of quality in ECE. In February, Governor Schweiker announced that he was convening an Early Care and Education Task Force to assess the health, safety, and school readiness needs of preschool-age children. His proposed 2002–2003 state budget also included $6 million to fund a three-year pilot program called "Keystone Stars." Under the program, the state DPW would develop and implement a voluntary quality-rating system for child-care providers throughout the state. Funding for the program has yet to be approved by the state legislature.

viding high-quality ECE services to low-income children. ECI's specific design and implementation put it in direct conflict with some of the state's other priorities, substantially undermining any hope that the state would ultimately take over funding responsibility for the initiative.

Inadequate Engagement of State Officials and Policymakers

Given the challenges facing ECI's state strategy, it was crucial that ECI's planners not only keep state policymakers and bureaucrats well informed about ECI, but also provide them a substantial opportunity to contribute to the initiative's design. In practice, ECI planners made some attempts to engage a few state officials, but they did not ensure that state policymakers had a full, substantive, and early role in the design process.

At the highest level of Pennsylvania politics, ECI's supporters included prominent contributors to the campaigns of Governor Tom Ridge, and those supporters brought ECI to the governor's attention. High-profile meetings with the governor, however, produced only general statements of support rather than a specific commitment of funding and legislative action. Some observers believe that ECI's supporters misunderstood the signals from the governor, giving an unduly optimistic interpretation to his general statements of support.

The engagement of state officials who were likely to bear direct responsibility for supervising a state-supported ECI may have been just as important as the commitment of the governor. Two state bureaucracies were the most obvious candidates for housing ECI. As a preschool program, ECI might have come under the jurisdiction of the Department of Education; as a child-care program, it might have come under the jurisdiction of the DPW, which supervises the existing system of child-care subsidies for low-income children. As noted in Chapter Two, one DPW official was consulted very early in ECI's process of conception, but he was not in a position to make key decisions about ECI. Neither Education nor DPW officials were prominently involved in the planning and design of ECI. The fact that neither department had previously shown interest in promoting high-quality ECE only made early engagement more important.

Among the state officials who were consulted by ECI's planners, some felt that their concerns were ignored. Others in Harrisburg, engaged only later in the process, felt that the initiative was presented to them as a completed package that they were expected to accept without having had the opportunity to provide substantive input on its design. The engagement by ECI seemed to them to be more about selling the initiative to the state than about taking the state's concerns seriously. In consequence, state officials often perceived the planners and business leaders who approached them about ECI as arrogant. Indeed, at least one state official felt that ECI's strategy was to embarrass the state into a funding commitment. Whether such an attitude was intended or not, its effect on state officials did not produce an eagerness to cooperate.

More-effective engagement with state policymakers in both the design and the implementation of ECI might have led to earlier warnings about the ways in which ECI came into conflict with other state priorities—conflicts that made a funding commitment from the state even less likely.

"Education" Became "Care"

ECI came into conflict with other state priorities partly because it came to be identified as a *child-care* initiative even though it had originally focused primarily on *education*. As originally conceived, ECI intended to serve most children in part-day, Head Start–like programs that would provide educational enrichment. One reason that Head Start has remained popular and politically viable for over 30 years is that it has always been viewed as an educational program rather than a child-care program. Many policymakers and voters perceive that education is intended primarily to benefit children and that child care is intended primarily to benefit parents. Public education is offered to all children universally, while child-care subsidies are often viewed as appropriate only for "deserving" low-income parents. In consequence, eligibility for child-care subsidies depends on meeting the requirements of welfare-reform laws. Because Head Start is viewed as an educational program, it has survived without tying eligibility to parental work.

ECI did not (initially) tie eligibility to parental work. It aimed to serve all at-risk children in the targeted neighborhoods, not only those who met welfare-reform requirements. But the shift to full-day services meant that the initiative became identified as a child-care program. Recognizing this, UW refocused ECI's state lobbying efforts specifically to DPW, which houses the major existing child-care subsidy programs for low-income families. Identified as a child-care program for low-income families rather than as an educational enrichment program, ECI entered the political world of welfare reform. In that context, fully subsidized service to children of nonworking parents—whatever its public-policy virtues—was politically problematic.

ECI and the State Subsidy System

To some extent in its design and to a greater extent in its implementation, ECI was less than fully compatible with the goals and operation of Pennsylvania's existing system of child-care subsidies for low-income families. Although the incompatibilities were not anticipated by ECI's designers and supporters when ECI was launched, they quickly became clear to some of the state officials who were asked to support ECI.

Pennsylvania operates two child-care subsidy programs for low-income parents. One program targets former welfare recipients and working-poor families; the other serves current TANF recipients participating in workfare and training-related activities.[4] Subsidies are the same for both programs, and parents are free to take their subsidies to any provider of their choice, regardless of whether the provider is a center, group child-care home, family child-care home,

---

[4]The program for former TANF recipients is funded primarily with federal CCDF block grant funds, which the state supplements. The program is administered at the local level by Child Care Information Service (CCIS) agencies that contract with the state DPW. In Allegheny County, the YWCA of Greater Pittsburgh serves as the CCIS agency. Parents must apply in person for CCIS subsidies at one of three offices in the county. The subsidy program for current TANF recipients participating in workfare and training-related activities is administered by county assistance offices and is funded by a combination of state and federal TANF funds. When a welfare recipient obtains a job, his/her children transfer from the TANF system to the CCIS system (even if the family is still receiving some TANF benefits). This transfer is achieved automatically because the TANF and CCIS client databases are linked. (Previously, former TANF recipients had to reapply for subsidies at the YWCA.)

or an unregulated provider (one serving three or fewer children, usually a relative or neighbor).

ECI first came into conflict with the state subsidy system when it failed to acknowledge the state's preference for parental choice in child care. ECI's business plan envisioned a bureaucratically controlled system with a carefully specified group of providers in each neighborhood. Moreover, the ECI state strategy initially assumed that ECI would get a line item in the state budget to fund it directly rather than through subsidies to parents. The conflict with the existing system of parental choice was especially acute early in ECI's operation, when the initiative sought both to require children to remain in their neighborhoods and to exclude children who were already served elsewhere. Although these restrictions were removed relatively early, ECI's efforts to acquire state support did not fully acknowledge the importance of parental choice until fairly late in ECI's existence.

Second, in practice if not in design, ECI came into conflict with the state's desire, via welfare reform, to induce parents on public assistance to enter the workforce. ECI's primary goal was to provide high-quality early education to low-income children regardless of whether their parents were working. The primary goal of the state child-care subsidy system, by contrast, is to provide incentives and means for parents receiving public assistance to move into the workforce. Encouraged by ECI planners to "dream big," many neighborhood leaders viewed ECI as an opportunity to provide high-quality ECE services to the neediest children in their community. Many of those children, however, were ineligible for state subsidies because their parents did not meet the requirements of Pennsylvania's welfare-reform law.

Children could be ineligible for a number of reasons, even if their families met the subsidy programs' income requirements. For example, children of single mothers could not obtain subsidies if their mothers were not working at least 20 hours per week, nor if their mothers had not filed for child support with the court system. Work requirements meant that many children were ineligible for subsidies during time that parents spent receiving drug or alcohol rehabilitation services. To many lead agencies and providers, these children were the most in need and therefore should receive priority for ECI programs.

But the state of Pennsylvania has not shown interest in subsidizing programs for children whose parents are not seeking work. Rather, state policymakers have made eligibility for child-care subsidies contingent on parents working in order to reward parents who work. Indeed, some state policymakers viewed ECI's subsidizing of children of nonworking parents as undermining the state welfare-reform policy.

SUSTAINABILITY IN THE ABSENCE OF A DIRECT STATE COMMITMENT

Conflicts with other state policy objectives surely made ECI's political objectives more difficult to achieve, but they became even more critical when ECI's sustainability strategy began depending more explicitly on the state's child-care subsidy system. In 1998, the first revision of the ECI business plan made two key changes that acknowledged the importance of the child-care subsidy system. First, recognizing that costs had been driven dramatically upward by the shift to full-day ECE services, the plan proposed to obtain the additional funds needed during ECI's first five years of operation by relying much more heavily on state subsidies. Nearly all of the anticipated $45 million increase in the five-year cost of ECI would be raised through existing state child-care subsidies, according to the plan. Second, the plan acknowledged that ECI's original political strategy, which had attempted to secure a specific commitment to new funding directed specifically to ECI, was unlikely to succeed, and that a more realistic sustainability strategy would involve the use and expansion of existing funding streams. Specifically, rather than seek a new line item in the state budget, ECI's supporters would lobby policymakers to raise subsidy reimbursement rates to 100 percent of the market rate for care (from the current 75 percent), and preferably to raise them even higher to cover the full cost of high-quality care. These changes meant that ECI's compatibility with the state child-care subsidy system was not only politically important for its long-term sustainability, but also operationally critical for ECI's fiscal viability in both the short and the long term.

In its early years of operation, ECI gave little attention to state subsidies as a substantial source of income, for several reasons. First, because the initiative originally was designed to focus primarily on part-day, Head Start–like educational services for children of unemployed parents, DPW's child-care subsidy system was not obviously relevant. Second, waiting lists for the largest state subsidy program were long. In many cases, families waited six to eight months from the time of application until children received subsidies. ECI's ability to tap these subsidies was therefore limited. In addition, although ECI's contracts with lead agencies nominally required that eligible parents apply for subsidies from the start, ECIM initially placed little emphasis on this source of revenue for providers. Indeed, this made some sense under the initial plan, which was committed to serving children regardless of whether their parents were working. According to our interviews, lead agencies were frequently told to get children enrolled in ECI and worry about getting their parents to apply for subsidies later. Moreover, because lead agencies (and parents) were receiving almost full reimbursements from ECI for each child's cost of care, they had little incentive to pursue state subsidies. Through 1998, revenue from state subsidies had contributed only 5 percent of ECI's total costs. Even into early 1999, only a small number of ECI children were receiving state subsidies.[5]

In February 1999, a major state policy change infused the child-care subsidy system with additional funding, and waiting lists were rapidly eliminated. Around the same time, UW management and ECIM began pressing lead agencies and providers to get parents to apply for subsidies.

But even full use of the state subsidy system would not have solved ECI's fiscal problems. Subsidy rates are 75 percent of the average market price of care for each type of service (center based, group child-care home, family child care, unregulated provider) in each county. In 1999, subsidies ranged from $20.60 to $25.80 per day, depending on the type of provider and the age of the child. These rates were far short of ECI's costs, which amounted to about $52 per child per day, more than double the average state subsidy rate for center-

---

[5]Underuse of state subsidies did not increase the total cost of the initiative; instead, it shifted costs from the state to ECI's donors.

based care in the county. Thus, ECI's high costs not only reduced its ability to serve large numbers of children, but also undermined its long-term sustainability.

In 1999 and 2000, UW made additional efforts to reduce ECI's costs and increase the proportion of ECI children receiving state subsidies. These efforts created conflicts with both ECIM and the lead agencies, for two reasons: They might undermine the commitment to quality, and they seemed to renege on the promises that had been made to the neighborhoods. Lead agencies had been sending the message throughout their neighborhoods that ECI programs were open to all children in need of care. But when UW insisted (in early 2000) that no new children be enrolled unless their parents had applied for state subsidies, lead agencies—as well as ECIM—saw this as breaking the promise to serve children most in need of high-quality care and education. When they began turning families without subsidies away, they fell under criticism from parents who felt betrayed. The lead agencies also felt that cost-cutting measures (e.g., lower re-imbursements for lead agency administrative expenses) would nega-tively impact their programs' quality of care, and high-quality care was what they were selling to parents. Lead agencies were especially frustrated because they had understood that ensuring long-term sustainability was not their concern but, rather, the responsibility of the ECI leaders and lobbyists who were appealing to the state.

In short, both the lead agencies and UW were in a bind created by the mistaken assumptions and unrealistic expectations of the origi-nal business plan. The lead agencies wanted to deliver on the promises made when ECI was launched; UW recognized that ECI was not sustainable without substantial changes. At this point, con-flicts and disappointment were inevitable.

CONCLUSION

When ECI was launched, the existing obstacles to its achieving sus-tainability through public funding from the state were substantial. Nevertheless, ECI undermined any chance it had for political success in two ways. First, it did not fully engage and acknowledge the con-cerns of state policymakers early enough in the design process. Sec-ond, and more fundamentally, the shift from part-day, Head Start–like educational services to full-day care and education brought ECI into conflict with the goals of the state's welfare-reform law. That conflict became an even more serious operational problem for ECI when it became more dependent on the state's existing child-care subsidy system. UW's struggles to reduce costs and make ECI compatible with the state subsidy system created major internal conflicts, undermined ECI's support in the neighborhoods, and, ultimately, were not successful enough to make ECI sustainable using existing or foreseeable levels of state subsidies.

Chapter Seven

LESSONS FOR THE FUTURE, ALTERNATIVE MODELS, AND PUBLIC-POLICY IMPLICATIONS

Many aspects of ECI—its theory of action, its administrative structure, the incentives it created, and its strategy for inducing the state to take over financial responsibility—suggest lessons for future large-scale private-public initiatives. This chapter discusses those lessons, presents some promising alternative models for the design of ECE initiatives, and addresses some of the public-policy implications of ECI's successes and failures.

LESSONS FOR FUTURE LARGE-SCALE PRIVATE-PUBLIC INITIATIVES

Focus on Clear Goals and Well-Defined Services

ECI's quality, scale, and community control goals often came into conflict with each other, especially when different stakeholders (e.g., ECIM, UW management, neighborhood leaders) prioritized these goals differently, or when different stakeholders (e.g., parents, neighborhood leaders, ECIM) defined quality differently. A narrower focus on a more limited number of goals may be a better approach, especially if goals are in tension with each other. A number of promising ECE initiatives in other communities (see next section) aim to provide high-quality ECE programs to children quickly by improving existing providers, rather than by promoting new centers through a community development effort involving substantial time and resources. This is not to say that an approach that places a high value on community involvement cannot succeed, but any such approach must recognize that scale-up may be slow and fitful.

Tensions among the ECI goals contributed to considerable disappointment in the neighborhoods involved in the initiative. Neighborhood leaders took ECI's encouragement to "dream big" seriously and were then frustrated when many of their dreams were constrained by the requirements of ECIM and UW. Real respect for the desires of local neighborhoods may require a less top-down approach to quality. Lead agencies were especially frustrated when financial constraints led UW to forbid them to enroll any further children who were ineligible for state subsidies. Many lead agencies had initiated ECE services with the specific intent of serving children who were poor but ineligible for subsidies. ECI leaders encouraged these expectations at the beginning and then found that they could not be fulfilled.

The desire to simultaneously serve multiple goals also contributed to a lack of clarity in ECI's specification of the services it aimed to provide. ECI originally assumed that most children would be served in part-day, preschool programs, but it offered a menu of different services that varied widely in cost. Because ECI's assumptions about the mix of services that would be wanted were incorrect, the cost-per-child estimates of its original business plan—which were critical for reaching the initiative's intended scale—proved to be substantially lower than the actual per-child costs.

Establish an Independent Board and a Clear Administrative Structure

ECIM's organizational structure was relatively straightforward below the level of the ECIM director, but the authority relationships above ECIM—among ECI's managers, UW management, funders, and the various advisory committees—were complex and ambiguous. This labyrinthine leadership structure made it difficult to resolve conflicts over ECI's goals and priorities, eventually leading to a power struggle between ECIM and UW, as well as frustration in the neighborhoods. An organizational structure must provide the opportunity for those within it to exercise strong leadership, both at the administrative level and the board level.

Adopt a Clean, Direct Theory of Action That Promotes Intended Goals

Even if ECI's administrative structure had functioned smoothly, it is not clear that ECI's goals could have been achieved given the theory of action implicit in the initiative's basic design. ECI's design created a complicated set of relationships among ECIM, lead agencies, providers, and parents. The theory of action created considerable distance between the funders and the children they hoped to serve by putting two layers of bureaucracy between the funders and the provider-family relationship. This arrangement ensured that administrative costs would be high; they proved to be far higher than the optimistic projections in the original business plan. In addition, the combination of a top-down quality assurance structure with the establishment of lead agencies as an intermediate level of the organizational structure made it difficult for ECI to increase capacity quickly and respond effectively to parental demand. An initiative that seeks to serve large numbers of children in a short period may require a less cumbersome structure that focuses more on the ultimate consumers of services.

Consider Demand, Supply, and Responses to Incentives

ECI's planners failed to appreciate that the ECE services demanded by parents and neighborhood agencies could be quite different from those envisioned in the original business plan. They seriously underestimated the demand for expensive, full-day services (rather than less-expensive, part-day programs) in the targeted communities. In part, this was because planners did not foresee the impact of welfare reform, which, in combination with a booming economy, put more low-income mothers in the workforce, thereby increasing the need for full-day services. But the demand for full-day services in new child-care centers probably would have occurred even in the absence of welfare reform, because parents and community agencies had every reason to ask for the most-comprehensive services when they were offered a range of choices, fully subsidized by ECI, and told to "dream big." This applied to capital improvements as well as the service mix: After ECIM and UW approved $800,000 to build a new center in one neighborhood, they should not have been surprised that most other community planning groups took notice and requested similar amounts.

The original planners also overestimated the extent to which existing providers would participate in ECI. Some existing providers were left out because the quality of their service was considered too low; in other cases, neighborhood agencies preferred to launch new providers, under their own control, rather than use existing providers. Others opted out because extra funding for quality improvements and training did not provide a strong enough incentive for them to participate. These providers were not receptive to monitoring and evaluation, nor did they wish to surrender control over program content, staffing, deciding which children to serve (e.g., infants/toddlers versus preschoolers), and other aspects of their operation. This was the case for several center-based providers that chose not to participate. It was the case for even more family child-care providers, who constitute a major part of the child-care market in low-income neighborhoods. Family child-care providers participated in ECI in only very small numbers.

In contrast, ECI was successful in working with existing Head Start providers. ECI provided the funding (which it secured through a state grant) and technical assistance necessary to get several Head Start centers licensed to provide full-day child care. It is important to note, however, that ECI did not consider most of these centers to be part of its system. They were not part of any community's plan, nor were they subject to ECI's quality monitoring system.

Include All Stakeholders

Although ECI's planners made efforts to include large numbers of stakeholders at some point in the process, they were less thorough in soliciting and appreciating the advice, concerns, and needs of three key groups: existing ECE service providers, parents, and state government officials. That is, ECI was extremely careful to listen to the perspectives of people from each geographic area (neighborhood) but was less effective in giving equal consideration to the interests of all stakeholders (see Table 4.1 for a description of stakeholder interests). More attention to existing service providers might have reduced costs and increased the pace of scale-up and the number of children served. More attention to parents might have provided early signals that the services demanded differed from those ECI sought to offer. More attention to state officials might have avoided some of ECI's conflicts with state policy and improved its prospects for long-term sustainability.

For planners of a major initiative, the key is to identify the stakeholders whose participation is critical and then ensure that they are included in relevant aspects of the initiative. In ECI's case, state policymakers were critical to long-term sustainability, so they should have been fully involved in the initial design of the initiative and its sustainability strategy. Similarly, existing ECE service providers were important, in this case because large numbers of children were already receiving their services. ECI would have had much better prospects for reaching its ambitious enrollment targets if it had sought to include these providers.

Start with an Independent Review

Foundation officers typically serve as independent reviewers for proposals that come from outside the foundation. When a foundation plays a large role in initiating a proposal, however, it should seek outside review by someone who (1) can identify flaws without fear of retribution, (2) is not a member of the original advocacy group, (3) has appropriate substantive expertise, and (4) will invest time and energy in the review commensurate with the importance of the project.

In ECI's case, the planners should be commended for their efforts to gain critical feedback from several directions. These efforts included the formation of a number of volunteer committees to ask hard questions, the pro bono use of expert consultants (from McKinsey & Co. and Ernst & Young) to assist with the business plan, and the commitment to an evaluation of outcomes (ultimately assigned to the SPECS team). Unfortunately, these efforts were not enough to identify and remedy a number of flaws in the business plan. The committees consisted largely of volunteers who were talented but very busy people lacking the time and (in most cases) the substantive expertise in ECE to conduct a thorough examination. Moreover, as friends and colleagues of ECI's planners, some of these people felt considerable social pressure to support ECI despite any misgivings they may have had. Indeed, extensive reliance on committees may be problematic if it diffuses responsibility, leaving no individual feeling responsible for ensuring the quality of the result. In contrast, ECI's pro bono consultants lacked specific expertise in ECE, community development, or philanthropy. And even expert consultants providing pro bono assistance may not be able to devote the same amount of time and attention they provide to their paying clients.[1] And as for the SPECS evaluation of outcomes, it was commissioned well after ECI's launch and thus could not serve to identify and remedy flaws in the original plan.

All in all, our interviews suggest that the ECI planning process created an atmosphere that implicitly discouraged or set aside objections, promoting uncritical optimism and an attitude of "if we build it, they will come." For example, some stakeholders told us that they recognized problems with the strategy for gaining state buy-in but felt pressured not to voice their concerns or had their concerns ignored. More than one interviewee described ECI as a "steamroller" that silenced all objections.

Make a Substantial Investment in Planning and Management

ECI was a large investment. Any decision to invest philanthropic funds on behalf of the community ought to be accompanied by a level of planning commensurate with the scale of the investment. Venture capitalists investing $59 million would probably expect a more rigorous business plan, which itself might involve a substantial investment. A large-scale philanthropic initiative might similarly be viewed as a staged investment that begins with a substantial business plan, proceeds with development of pilot programs, and only then moves on to large-scale investment and implementation.

An ambitious plan should have a sufficiently tested model to emulate. The original planners thought that they were planning and implementing something that had been tested on a small scale—high-quality ECE programs, such as Perry Preschool, had been implemented in various places over the preceding 35 years. But rather

---

[1]Indeed, UW may have recognized this when they chose not to rely on pro bono assistance for revisions to the business plan, instead contracting with Dickerson & Mangus, Ink.

than simply attempting to recreate the Perry Preschool Project (or any other pre-existing ECE program), ECI was attempting to create a new system for high-quality ECE, directed by neighborhood agencies under the supervision of an intensive quality assurance process. Neither the effectiveness and efficiency of the quality monitoring system nor the ability of community groups to plan, establish, and operate ECE programs (in a short, three-to-five year timeframe) had been demonstrated. In sum, ECI attempted to implement a new system on a large scale that had not been piloted on a smaller scale.

As mentioned above, an initiative on this scale should be expected to have its own empowered board to exercise ultimate leadership over major policy decisions (and especially to resolve conflicts among competing goals). Venture capitalists making an investment of comparable scale might insist on a leadership team that includes a CEO with entrepreneurial experience as well as general management experience. ECI would not have passed this test. It did not have its own board, nor did it ever have a leader who was given the authority of a CEO to make operational decisions for ECI. Moreover, as a result of personnel changes, some of ECI's administrators were given responsibilities that extended beyond their experience and expertise. Those involved in managing ECI (both ECIM and UW management) were talented people with expertise in a number of areas, but ECI lacked a CEO who had experience in managing large endeavors and in starting them from scratch (as well as an administrative structure that permitted the exercise of strong leadership).

Make Sure Bold Visions Are Backed Up by Hardheaded Plans That Acknowledge Political and Policy Realities

We do not wish to discourage big dreams, but those who dream big will need careful, hardheaded plans to bring those dreams to fruition.

Planners should recognize that the existence of a strong societal benefit/cost ratio (in ECI's case, inferred from the Perry Preschool results) often is not enough to induce policymakers and politicians to support an initiative. Moreover, the mere creation of high-quality programs does not ensure that consumers will recognize them as being of high quality. Planners should acknowledge the existing political and policy landscape and should include key policymakers (e.g., state officials) in the development of the vision and plan, recognizing that the plan may need to change to meet the demands of competing policies. This is not to say that planners must endorse existing policies with which they disagree; but, if their initiative requires political support, they should avoid unnecessary conflicts with competing policies.

Planners and funders should also carefully consider the match between their goals and those of the intermediaries they choose to house their initiatives. In ECI's case, UW had important advantages in terms of its fundraising ability and its credibility across the community. Its institutional weaknesses were a relative inexperience in operating programs (versus distributing funds) and a culture that did not encourage risk-taking. While the original planners and UW board members realized that UW would not be an ideal permanent home for ECI, they thought that it would suffice as a temporary home until the initiative could be spun off as an independent organization. Indeed, there were no other obvious candidates to house ECI during its inaugural period. Despite its weaknesses, UW might have been a successful incubator of ECI if it had established a stronger administrative structure and if ECIM had been more happily integrated into UW. In practice, UW did not work well for ECI because the administrative structure was complex and because UW management and ECIM did not work well together.

ALTERNATIVE MODELS FOR THE DESIGN OF ECE INITIATIVES

Whereas the lessons discussed above should be generally useful for large-scale privately led initiatives in the future, questions remain about the specific design of ECE initiatives. How might a future initiative, in Pittsburgh or elsewhere, be designed to effectively achieve the implementation of high-quality ECE services on a large scale? Here we briefly describe four promising ECE initiatives operating in other communities. These descriptions are intended to illustrate alternative programs designed to increase the quality and quantity of ECE services for low-income children. Formal evaluation results are as yet available for only one of these programs, but we believe that each program represents a promising approach that funders, policymakers, and ECE practitioners may wish to consider.[2]

The Chicago Child-Parent Center Program

Like the Perry Preschool Project, the Chicago Child-Parent Center (CPC) program is a high-quality ECE effort with a rigorous evaluation component that has followed participating children into their post–high school years and has found lasting positive impacts. What sets the CPC program apart from other model programs, however, is that it is a relatively large-scale effort, serving between 3,000 and 5,000 children each year.[3] Launched in 1967 and funded primarily with federal Title I grants, the program is administered by the Chicago Public Schools. It consists of 24 early education centers, each serving 130 to 210 low-income, largely minority children. The average cost per child for one year of preschool services is an estimated $4,520 (in 1998 dollars) (Karoly et al., 2001).

The centers provide three hours of preschool daily for three- and four-year-old children, as well as kindergarten services. They provide children with intensive learning activities with a focus on language development and the acquisition of pre-reading skills. In addition, children receive health and nutrition services (Reynolds, 2000). Like ECI centers, each center has a highly trained staff, keeps class sizes small (a maximum of 17 per preschool classroom), and has high staff-to-child ratios (like ECI, about one staff member per eight children in preschool classrooms, and one per 12 children in kindergarten classrooms). Staff receive regular in-service training. In addition, the CPC program requires substantial parent participation. Many of the participating children receive follow-up services (at a lower level of intensity and cost) during their first several years of elementary school (Reynolds, 2000).

---

[2]The description of the Chicago Child-Parent Center program is based on published reports; the descriptions of the other three programs are based primarily on interviews with program directors and funders.

[3]The prototypical large-scale ECE program, of course, is Head Start. However, Head Start's impact on children over the long term has not been well studied. Moreover, while Head Start programs vary widely in their level of quality (U.S. General Accounting Office, 1997; Zigler and Muenchow, 1992), the CPC program has maintained a high level of quality across all 24 of its centers.

Program evaluators have tracked samples of participating and non-participating children who completed kindergarten in 1986, finding lasting positive program effects. Program participants spent significantly fewer years in special education than did children in the comparison group; they also were more likely to have graduated from high school and had obtained more total years of education by age 20. Their rates of petition to juvenile court were also significantly lower (Karoly et al., 2001; Reynolds et al., 2001; Reynolds, 2000). In addition, a recent cost-benefit analysis suggests that the benefits of the CPC program to government and society exceed its costs by a substantial margin: Researchers estimate that each $1 spent has produced almost $4 in benefits to government, society, and program participants, a ratio comparable to that demonstrated by Perry Preschool (Karoly et al., 2001).

While the CPC program shares many goals with ECI, there are significant differences. First, CPC does not employ the community-driven approach that was central to ECI. It is operated by the city school district and was designed by school administrators and teachers. Although the centers have close links with their respective communities, community representatives play a minimal role in program design and operation. Getting centers operational and scaled up (in the late 1960s, when the program was initiated) took relatively little time, and the program did not become embroiled in neighborhood politics.

Because the centers are operated by the school district, programs are more closely connected to the elementary schools than are most ECI programs. (A strong connection was made between the Braddock ECI programs and the local school district, but not elsewhere.) While largely dependent on federal funding, the centers benefit substantially from the administrative experience, educational expertise, and resources that the schools can offer, including the availability of suitable physical facilities. In addition, CPC is clearly identified as an educational program (rather than child care) and therefore can avoid some of the political conflicts and eligibility disputes associated with child care under welfare reform.

Child Care Matters in Southeastern Pennsylvania

The Child Care Matters (CCM) initiative in Southeastern Pennsylvania is based at United Way of Southeastern Pennsylvania (UWSEPA) in partnership with four other local nonprofit organizations.[4] CCM's major goal is to expand the availability of high-quality ECE services for children in Philadelphia and surrounding communities, with special attention to services for low-income families. The William Penn Foundation provided $14 million for the first six years of the initiative, which began in July 1997. UWSEPA raised an additional $3 million and intends to raise an additional $750,000.

A management team consisting of a top administrator from each of the five partner agencies is responsible for operational and strategic decisions. The director of CCM, who is on the staff at UWSEPA, leads the management team and oversees day-to-day management of the initiative. CCM also has a 25-member governing committee that includes representatives from UWSEPA's board, the local business community, various social service agencies, area school districts, churches, community colleges, and similar organizations.

Under its Accreditation Project, CCM works with child-care centers and family child-care homes in two Philadelphia neighborhoods, its ultimate goal being to achieve NAEYC accreditation (or NAFCC accreditation for family child-care providers). Both neighborhoods have large numbers of young children, and both have providers with close ties to some of CCM's partner agencies. Interested providers in these neighborhoods receive intensive technical assistance and funding to improve the quality of their programs. Technical assistance is provided by "cluster leaders," experienced child-care professionals with a thorough understanding of the accreditation process. Each cluster leader works intensely with up to five providers. Funding for quality improvements, including facility renovations, equipment, and supplies, ranges from $40,000 to $60,000 per center

---

[4]These are the Delaware Valley Association for the Education of Young Children, the Philadelphia Early Childhood Collaborative, the Delaware Valley Child Care Council, and Philadelphia Citizens for Children and Youth.

and is approximately $5,000 per family child-care home. Sixteen centers and 25 homes are currently participating in the project.[5]

CCM leaders have realized that many providers in these two neighborhoods are a long way from offering a level of care sufficient for accreditation. For providers for which accreditation is not yet a realistic goal, CCM staff provide technical assistance and funding for more-basic quality improvements. Beginning with the licensing standards they must meet, these providers work on taking incremental steps to improving their quality of care. Twelve centers and 35 homes are currently participating in this part of the initiative.

In addition, CCM has helped 45 family child-care homes become registered with the state and licensed with the city of Philadelphia. Several of these providers are included among the 35 family child-care homes that are making basic quality improvements, and some are working toward NAFCC accreditation.

All of the providers involved with CCM in these neighborhoods are eligible to participate in the T.E.A.C.H. (Teacher Education and Compensation Helps) Early Childhood Project. Through T.E.A.C.H., CCM provides scholarships to child-care workers who further their education in child development. Many use the scholarship to obtain a Child Development Associate credential. Participating child-care workers receive a salary increase or bonus, funded through T.E.A.C.H., with each year of course work they complete.

CCM also provides a "quality supplement"—a funding supplement for each child enrolled who is receiving a public subsidy—to any center or family child-care provider in the four-county region[6] that is or becomes NAEYC or NAFCC accredited. The objective is to assist providers who attain this level of quality and to provide an incentive for others who are accredited to accept low-income children. CCM staff estimate that these quality supplements enable 250 to 300 low-income children per quarter to receive high-quality care.

---

[5]Impressed with CCM's accomplishments in this area, UWSEPA is now urging all ECE providers that receive UWSEPA funding (separate from the CCM initiative) to begin working toward accreditation. Beginning next year, UWSEPA funding will be contingent on these agencies being able to demonstrate that they are taking steps to become NAEYC or NAFCC accredited.

[6]These include Philadelphia, Chester, Delaware, and Montgomery counties.

CCM differs from ECI in several important respects. First, it focuses on improving the quality of care offered by existing providers and has not attempted to create a new system of services or build new child-care centers. To a much greater extent than ECI, CCM has "gone where the kids are." Second, in providing technical assistance and funding to specific providers interested in improving their quality, CCM started on a smaller scale, targeting only two neighborhoods. Third, CCM's administrative structure and theory of action are simpler than ECI's, because CCM works directly with providers. And like the CPC program, CCM has not attempted to join its model of high-quality care and education with community-driven program design and administration.

Focus on Our Future in York County, Pennsylvania

A third promising model is the Focus on Our Future (FOF) initiative in York County. Like Philadelphia's CCM, FOF has focused primarily on improving the quality of care in existing child-care centers and family child-care homes, as well as on increasing the number of slots in these programs.

The seeds for FOF were planted in the mid-1990s, when the Heinz Endowments and Pew Charitable Trusts gave grants to the Community Commonwealth Foundation to fund initiatives throughout Pennsylvania to improve services for children. The York Foundation successfully secured funding to serve children in York County. Three years of planning ensued, as the York Foundation worked with UW of York County and other interested organizations to develop a plan for action.

The result of this process was FOF, which formally began in January 1997. FOF is an initiative of UW of York County, but UW has partnered with the Penn State–York campus and Child Care Consultants, Inc. (the Child Care Information Service for York County) to administer the initiative. Overseeing FOF staff at UW is a steering committee consisting of area business leaders, philanthropists, educators, child-care advocates, and others.

One major effort of FOF has been to increase the number of local child-care workers who are trained in child development and education. FOF has sponsored various training and continuing education opportunities. A second important goal has been to improve the quality of care offered by existing providers and to help these providers become accredited. In its first three years, FOF provided "quality enhancement funds" to 22 centers and 21 family child-care homes in York County. FOF staff have given priority to programs that are pursuing accreditation, and, as of this year, only programs that are either accredited or near the end of the accreditation process can receive grants. Also in its first three years, FOF provided technical assistance and funding that enabled six centers and four home-based providers in York County to become accredited.

The FOF experience has convinced the local UW board of the value of accreditation. The board recently decided that it will require all of its funded agencies that provide child care and early education services to be accredited with NAEYC or NAFCC by December 2002.

FOF mirrors CCM in its strategy to work with existing providers and other existing organizations. Unlike ECI, FOF has not emphasized the building of new centers. Nor has it employed the community-driven approach that was central to ECI. And like CCM, its administrative structure and theory of action are simpler than those of ECI.

Focus on Quality in Chicago

A final model worth considering is the Focus on Quality (FOQ) initiative in Chicago. Launched in 1994 by the Robert R. McCormick Tribune Foundation, FOQ aims to raise the quality of existing child-care providers, with an emphasis on those in Chicago's low-income neighborhoods. FOQ aims to get existing providers accredited or on the path to accreditation. The foundation contracted with four established nonprofit organizations to help providers become NAEYC or NAFCC accredited: The Big Shoulders Fund of the Archdiocese of Chicago's Office of Catholic Education, the Ecumenical Child Care Network, the Center for Early Education Leadership at National-Louis University, and the Chicago Metropolitan Association for the Education of Young Children (CMAEYC). All of these organizations have considerable experience providing training and technical assistance to child-care providers and their staff.

With funding from the foundation, these four organizations recruit existing providers in several Chicago neighborhoods. They work with centers and with some family child-care providers, although reaching this latter group of providers has proved to be difficult. An interested center applies for FOQ funding and technical assistance. FOQ staff from CMAEYC or one of the other agencies then visit the center to assess how much improvement it requires to meet NAEYC standards. Next, staff sit down with the center's director and develop a detailed plan for improvement. Needed improvements for accreditation can be new curricula and materials, new equipment, repairs, training of teachers and caregiving staff, or playground renovations. FOQ funds many of these improvements, offers technical assistance during each step of the accreditation process, and provides or arranges training.

Prior to FOQ, only 19 centers in the city were NAEYC accredited, and most of them did not serve low-income children. FOQ has helped 103 child-care centers in Chicago become accredited over a five-year period and is assisting another 62 centers that are in the accreditation process. Most of these centers are in low-income neighborhoods. FOQ staff have provided a smaller number of family child-care homes with accreditation assistance. CMAEYC and the other agencies are now focusing their efforts on providers that offer lower-quality services.

Over five years, the McCormick Tribune Foundation spent nearly $11 million on this effort and an additional $15 million on related activities to improve the quality of ECE services in Chicago. These related activities included expanded training opportunities for child-care workers, a public awareness campaign targeted to low-income parents (regarding the importance of high quality ECE), a program to help ECE advocacy groups build their organizational and management capacities, and a sustained effort to press city and state policymakers to increase funding for ECE programs (including the state's child-care subsidy system). To implement these programs, the foundation has contracted with several other local nonprofit agencies.

Impressed by FOQ's achievements in helping so many providers become accredited, the city of Chicago recently initiated the Chicago Accreditation Partnership (CAP). A partnership of the city, the McCormick Tribune Foundation, and other local funders, CAP aims to continue FOQ beyond its initial five years and broaden the reach of its accreditation efforts. In total, the partners have pooled $16 million (including $5 million from the city) to fund the accreditation of more centers and family child-care homes.

Unlike ECI, FOQ focused on raising the quality of existing providers, thereby serving a large number of children in just five years. Like the other programs described here, FOQ did not use a community-driven approach. Rather, it relied heavily on nonprofit agencies with considerable experience serving ECE programs, and these agencies dealt directly with program directors and their staff.

Concluding Thoughts on Alternative Models

These programs by no means constitute the full array of promising ECE initiatives. Nevertheless, each suggests an alternative approach to scaling up high-quality ECE services. In contrast to ECI, each program has a narrower focus on a more limited number of goals. None places much emphasis on the goal of community control, and most focus on existing providers, thereby making the scale-up process more straightforward and usually faster.

Future large-scale ECE initiatives might consider any of these possibilities, or might instead consider a parent-centered approach. For example, planners might choose to distribute funds as quality-focused supplements to the existing state subsidy system. Parents would be permitted to use "quality vouchers" at any provider that met a designated quality standard. If an existing standard, such as NAEYC accreditation, is considered insufficient, a separate quality monitoring system could be established to identify high-quality providers and enforce standards. Additional grants might be available to providers seeking to improve their quality in order to become eligible for the "quality vouchers."[7]

We do not mean to suggest that pursuing a community-driven approach is necessarily bad. But funders, program planners, and policymakers need to understand that community-driven processes inevitably take time. Moreover, communities may have desires and

---

[7]An approach that builds on the existing subsidy system, however, cannot address the quality of ECE for children who are ineligible for subsidies.

interests that differ from those of the planners; in consequence, an approach that takes the community's desires seriously must be prepared to accept results that may differ from those the planners and funders originally intended. An approach that simultaneously aims to permit community control and to impose top-down bureaucratic control may well lead to disappointment on all sides.

Although we found no examples among the initiatives described above, there may be alternative models that would both take the community's desires more seriously and provide more appropriate incentives, permitting communities to "dream big" while controlling costs and ensuring quality. In addition, it is worth pointing out that parent-centered models are implicitly community based, because they are driven by the desires of the parents of the community.

IMPLICATIONS FOR PUBLIC POLICY

As ECI's planners recognized, inducing large and sustained changes in the ECE universe requires public action. State and federal policymakers have the ability to exercise substantial influence over conditions in the ECE market, if they choose to do so. Here we briefly address a few broad public-policy issues raised by ECI's successes and failures. For example, what methods might policymakers use to promote quality in the existing system? Can policymakers address the problem that high-quality ECE may be underappreciated or not recognized by parents? How should policymakers think about public investments at different points in the life cycle, and should ECE be regarded as comparable to K–12 schooling? ECI may yet be able to make further important contributions to the public interest by raising these issues for public debate.

Promoting the Demand for Quality

Evidence suggests that parents do not have a high demand for high-quality ECE services, at least as understood by ECE experts (Blau, 2001). This may be because they do not know how to judge quality. Studies have found that parents tend to overestimate the quality of child-care providers (Walker, 1991; Cryer and Burchinal, 1995). In addition, parents may define quality differently than do the experts, placing a high value on familiarity and intimacy. Research has demonstrated that convenience, familiarity, and reliability are very important to parents (Sonenstein, 1991). Low-income parents are especially likely to choose unregulated care provided by neighbors and relatives (Blau, 2001). Some unregulated providers agree (illegally) to share a portion of the subsidy payments with parents, thereby supplementing the parents' incomes and giving them additional reason to choose unregulated care.

Because parents ultimately decide child-care arrangements for their children, their preferences are critical. Indeed, the success of any initiative that aims to deliver high-quality ECE requires some level of parental demand for quality.

But the preferences and knowledge base of parents are not set in stone. Policymakers (and local planners) may be able to increase the demand for high-quality services through public awareness campaigns and parent education efforts. Such efforts could include education about the long-term benefits of high-quality ECE, the characteristics of service that are good indicators of high quality, and the relevance of external quality certifications, such as NAEYC accreditation.

Pennsylvania may soon take a small step toward improving the information available to parents on the quality of ECE providers. Governor Schweiker's proposed 2002–2003 state budget includes $6 million to fund a three-year pilot program called "Keystone Stars." Under the program, the state DPW would develop and implement a voluntary quality-rating system for child-care providers. Participating providers would be assigned one of three levels of quality (based on levels of staff training and education, staff-to-child ratios, and related quality measures) and would be eligible for incentive funding and technical assistance to reach the next level. As of this writing, funding for the program has yet to be approved by the state legislature.

Quality Supplements

In addition to trying to influence parental demand, policymakers may seek to raise quality directly. One increasingly popular approach to raising the quality of ECE services is a tiered subsidy system. Under such a system, each provider receives a per-child subsidy based on the provider's level of quality. Higher-quality providers receive a higher subsidy rate. This approach is intended to give providers an incentive to improve their quality. Already, 26 states and the District of Columbia have instituted tiered subsidy systems (Education Week, 2002). The standards used to determine higher versus lower levels of quality vary, but several states have adopted NAEYC accreditation as evidence of the highest-quality care, with subsidy rates increasing as more NAEYC standards (in terms of group sizes, staff-to-child ratios, etc.) are achieved. To be effective, this approach requires a more rigorous monitoring system than most states, including Pennsylvania, have employed.

Substantial increases in federal and state funding for child care have gone largely toward increasing the number of children who receive subsidized care. But states have the discretion to use these funds to raise subsidy amounts, thereby making high-quality care more affordable for low-income families. Currently, subsidies in Pennsylvania pay for approximately 75 percent of the average market price for child-care services in each county. This does not come close to covering the cost of the kinds of high-quality programs that ECI sought to establish. Over the past five years, the state substantially increased the amount of funding for subsidized care in order to serve many more children, but it only modestly increased the subsidy rates per child. Tied to quality, increases in subsidy levels could induce existing providers to improve quality and make high-quality ECE services available to larger numbers of low-income children.

In Pennsylvania, reimbursement rates vary based on the age of the child (with younger children receiving a higher subsidy because their care is more costly) and the type of care (with group care homes and centers receiving a higher subsidy than family child-care homes). Family child-care homes serving three or fewer children also receive a higher subsidy if they become registered. Subsidy rates do not vary according to any measure of the quality of ECE provided. Only recently has the state begun to appropriate some funding for quality improvements in child-care programs. So far, this funding has been relatively insignificant compared with that of other states. But Pennsylvania state policymakers are now considering a tiered reimbursement approach that would increase the state's investment in high-quality ECE.

Professional Development for Providers

Greater public investments in the education and training of ECE workers might serve as a useful complement to a quality supplement policy. Policymakers could create incentives for providers to enroll their workers in continuing education programs in child development and early education. Pennsylvania (as well as many other states) has in fact increased funding for professional development opportunities in recent years. For example, Pennsylvania state policymakers recently decided to subsidize the T.E.A.C.H. program (described above, in the subsection on the Child Care Matters initiative). Under T.E.A.C.H., ECE workers across the state can apply for funding to help pay for tuition and other costs associated with college-level classes in child development or early education.

Education, Care, and Work Incentives

Converting the existing child-care subsidy system to a tiered system may induce an improvement in the quality of many existing providers, thereby providing long-term educational and social benefits to many low-income children. Unfortunately, however, it could leave unaffected a substantial number of low-income children who are ineligible for subsidies because their parents do not meet the requirements of state and federal welfare-reform laws. As a number of the neighborhood agencies affiliated with ECI recognized, some of the children who are most in need of high-quality services may be ineligible for welfare-related subsidies.

Head Start avoids this dilemma by making eligibility open to all low-income children, regardless of parental employment status. But Head Start is a part-day preschool program that has never been funded at levels sufficient to enroll all eligible children. As long as the primary method for subsidizing ECE for low-income children is subsidies tied to TANF eligibility, a substantial number of low-income children will be left out of the system. This is because in Pennsylvania and across the country, the primary objective of the child-care subsidy is to help welfare mothers obtain employment, rather than to provide high-quality services to at-risk children. Indeed, the fact that the primary objective is to create an employment incentive also explains why subsidies in Pennsylvania and elsewhere are available without regard to the quality of the ECE services provided. The federal welfare-reform law requires that states administer their child-care grants as vouchers that can be used at any licensed ECE provider or any provider that is exempt from licensing (including relatives and babysitters).

Indeed, the combination of the enduring popularity of Head Start and the ambivalence about public funding for full-day child care suggests a kind of schizophrenia in public policy related to ECE. Education is considered a public responsibility, whereas child care is not. For a program that combines both care and education, the label that is attached may determine political viability.

The economist David Blau (2001) argues that child-care subsidies should be divorced from employment policy and tied instead to child-care quality. Blau demonstrates empirically that child-care subsidies have only a small effect on the employment decisions of mothers, but he points out that they might be designed to have a substantial effect on the quality of services provided to children. He argues that the empirical evidence suggests that "using child care subsidies to address the employment problem is likely to worsen the child care problem by increasing the use of low-quality care" (Blau, 2001, p. 231).

Many policymakers and voters resist the idea of separating child-care subsidies from employment requirements. They often see employment requirements not only as a way to provide appropriate incentives to welfare mothers, but also as a way to distinguish between "deserving" and "undeserving" poor in the distribution of government benefits. Whether this latter purpose is appropriate is a matter of basic values, such as fairness and justice, and is not easily susceptible to empirical policy analysis. But policymakers may wish to consider the costs to society of a child-care policy that focuses on the deservingness of parents rather than the welfare of children.

ECI COST MODELS

This appendix presents four models that we developed in order to conduct a cost analysis of ECI. We created cost models to describe (1) the original ECI plan, (2) what the original plan would have looked like if the planners had accurately predicted the actual service mix, (3) what the original plan would have looked like if the planners had accurately predicted the actual service mix *and* had recognized that operating costs would be largely fixed instead of variable, and (4) actual ECI costs. All three models estimate the full economic cost of ECI. Most of this cost was borne by donors (both in the plan and in actuality), but small amounts were subsidized by government funds and parent co-payments.

THE ORIGINAL ECI PLAN

Table A.1 depicts how the original planners estimated total costs and the cost per child for ECI. The planners envisioned six possible types of service from which neighborhoods would choose: Head Start–like classrooms, new child-care centers, existing child-care centers, new family child-care (FCC) homes, existing FCC homes, and literacy/school readiness programs. Head Start–like and literacy programs were expected to provide half-day service; the other four types were expected to provide full-day service. Once operational, all programs were expected to serve children for a full year (approximately 260 days). Planners expected that each new Head Start–like classroom would serve 32 children; each new center, 85 children; and each FCC home, four children.

Annual operating costs were based on an assumed cost per child enrolled for each type of service (adjusted for the number of months the child is served). For example, the planners estimated that the operating cost per child for new centers would be $7,280 in year one. For each type of service, operating costs were calculated by multiplying the cost per child by the adjusted number of children enrolled. The operating cost per child was assumed to be constant, regardless of the number of children enrolled. Summing operating costs for all service types gave the total operating cost.

Annual capital costs were based on an assumed cost for new classrooms, new centers, and new FCC homes. The planners assumed that existing centers and FCC homes would receive operating funds but not capital funds. (In reality, existing centers and homes received a small amount of ECI funding for capital improvements.) Summing capital costs for all three types of facilities gave the total capital cost. We converted capital costs to a per-child basis to facilitate comparison.

In the original plan, capital costs were not amortized, but we amortized capital costs over a 15-year period at a 7 percent interest rate. Capital costs were incurred for a variety of items, ranging from tables and chairs to major building and playground renovations and construction. The useful life of each of these items will obviously vary, but we lacked detailed data to disaggregate total capital costs into categories. Thus, we assumed an average useful life of 15 years over which to amortize capital costs. We also adopted 7 percent as a reasonable market rate for amortizing these kinds of capital costs.[1] To test the sensitivity of our results to these choices, we calculated costs using shorter and longer time periods, as well as lower and higher interest rates. We found that the choice of rate and time period does not have a substantial impact on the resulting cost per child.

In the original plan, central administrative costs were not based on enrollment but were derived roughly from expectations about the number of staff that would be needed. The original planners viewed these costs as being largely fixed, although there was some acknowl-

---

[1]We based our choice of interest rate in part on input from established center-based providers.

edgment that eventually more staff would be needed as more neighborhoods were engaged.

Summing the total operating cost, total capital cost, and central administrative cost gives the total cost per year. In Table A.1, we show the total cost both with capital costs amortized and without amortization. We calculate the cost per child (per year) using the total with amortization. We divide this value by the total number of children enrolled (adjusted for number of months served). Hence, in year three (in practice, the last full year of the initiative and the last year for which we were able to obtain cost data), the total cost per child was expected to be $4,407. Operating costs were to account for 90 percent of the total expected cost per child, and administrative costs represent only 6 percent.

To produce estimates of cost per child-hour, we multiplied the adjusted number of children enrolled by the average number of hours in care per day for each type of service. In the original plan, children in part-day programs were expected to receive an average of 3.5 hours of service each day. (This is generally the amount of time that children spend in Head Start centers in Allegheny County.) The original plan assumed that children would receive about 9 hours of care in full-day programs. However, we chose to use an estimate based on the actual experience of ECI children so that our cost-per-child-hour estimates would be comparable to those we calculated using actual cost data (described below). For full-day programs, we assumed an average of 10 hours per day. We based this assumption on what several lead agency representatives and ECI center directors told us. Because neither UW nor ECIM collected detailed data on the number of hours of service provided, these were the only estimates we could obtain. (And our interviewees have told us that virtually all ECI children received full-day care.) Finally, we multiplied the product of these two variables (children enrolled, adjusted for number of months served; and the number of hours per day of service) by 260, the average number of days of care provided by a full-year ECI program, to get the total number of hours of service per year. By dividing the total (amortized) cost by the total number of hours of service, we obtained the planned cost per child-hour, which is $3.02 in year three.

Table A.1

Planned ECI Costs

Year[a]	1996	1997	1998	1999	2000	2001
	0	1	2	3	4	5
Children enrolled						
Head Start–like classrooms		192	416	1,248	1,984	2,976
New child-care centers		0	85	170	170	595
Existing centers		50	100	150	200	240
New FCC homes		40	228	468	788	1,268
Existing homes		10	20	60	80	100
Literacy/readiness programs		125	250	500	750	2,400
Total		417	1,099	2,596	3,972	7,579
Children enrolled, adjusted for number of months served						
Head Start–like classrooms		96	304	832	1,616	2,480
New child-care centers		0	43	128	170	383
Existing centers		25	75	125	175	220
New FCC homes		20	134	348	628	1,068
Existing homes		5	15	40	70	90
Literacy/readiness programs		63	188	500	750	2,400
Total		209	759	1,973	3,409	6,641
Child capacity added each year (number of slots)						
Head Start–like classrooms		192	224	832	736	992
New child-care centers		85	85	170	425	0
New FCC homes		60	282	360	480	600
Operating costs per child[b]						
Head Start–like classrooms		3,900	4,000	4,120	4,240	4,320
New child-care centers		7,280	7,500	7,725	7,950	8,175
Existing centers		5,720	5,890	6,060	6,240	6,400
New FCC homes		5,400	5,560	5,725	5,900	6,075
Existing homes		3,800	3,900	4,015	4,135	4,260
Literacy/readiness programs		1,000	1,000	1,000	1,000	1,000

Table A.1 (continued)

Year[a]	1996	1997	1998	1999	2000	2001
	0	1	2	3	4	5
Capital cost per child capacity						
Head Start–like classrooms		759	759	759	759	759
Child-care centers		5,000	5,000	5,000	5,000	5,000
FCC homes		200	200	200	200	200
Capital costs						
Head Start–like classrooms		145,800	170,100	631,800	558,900	753,300
Child-care centers		425,000	425,000	850,000	2,125,000	0
FCC homes		12,000	56,400	72,000	96,000	120,000
Total capital costs		582,800	651,500	1,553,800	2,779,900	873,300
Amortized capital costs[c]		63,988	135,520	306,118	611,336	707,220
Operating costs						
Head Start–like classrooms		374,400	1,216,000	3,427,840	6,851,840	10,713,600
New child-care centers		0	318,750	984,938	1,351,500	3,126,938
Existing centers		143,000	441,750	757,500	1,092,000	1,408,000
New FCC homes		108,000	745,040	1,992,300	3,705,200	6,488,100
Existing homes		19,000	58,500	160,600	289,450	383,400
Literacy/readiness programs		62,500	187,500	500,000	750,000	2,400,000
Total operating costs		706,900	2,967,540	7,823,178	14,039,990	24,520,038
Central administrative costs	133,125	518,991	551,540	563,775	563,775	599,525
Total	133,125	1,808,691	4,170,580	9,940,753	17,383,665	25,992,863
Total with amortization	133,125	1,289,879	3,654,600	8,693,071	15,215,101	25,826,783
Cost per child-year, with amortization						
Children-years served		208.5	758.0	1,972.5	3,409.0	6,640.5
Capital		307	179	155	179	107
Capital as % of total		5	4	4	4	3
Administrative		2,489	728	286	165	90
Administrative as % of total		40	15	6	4	2
Operating		3,390	3,915	3,966	4,119	3,692
Operating as % of total		55	81	90	92	95
Total		6,186	4,821	4,407	4,463	3,889

Table A.1 (continued)

Year[a]	1996	1997	1998	1999	2000	2001
	0	1	2	3	4	5
Cost per child-hour, with amortization						
Child-hours per year[d]		274,235	1,140,165	2,877,420	4,864,860	9,018,100
Operating		2.58	2.60	2.72	2.89	2.72
Capital		0.23	0.12	0.11	0.13	0.08
Administrative		1.89	0.48	0.20	0.12	0.07
Total		4.70	3.21	3.02	3.13	2.86

[a]The plan expected year one of implementation to be July 1996 through June 1997, but year one actually began January 1997. (June through December 1996 was a planning period.)

[b]Includes inflation, which is 3 percent per year, but then rounded off.

[c]Capital costs are amortized over a 15-year period at a 7 percent interest rate.

[d]Assumes 12 months of service equals 260 days, part-day care averages 3.5 hours per day, and full-day care averages 10 hours per day.

PLANNED COSTS BASED ON THE ACTUAL SERVICE MIX

Table A.2 presents a model that shows what the costs in the original plan would have looked like if the planners had accurately predicted the actual service mix (types of services used, such as new centers, existing centers, classrooms, family child-care homes, etc.). In this model, we used the same cost drivers (i.e., operating cost per child for each type of service and capital cost per child capacity for each type of facility) that were assumed in the original plan. We also used the same total enrollment projected by the original plan, but here we allocated this enrollment across service types based on the actual service mix. The enrollment numbers shown, and used in the analysis, have been adjusted for the expected number of months that children would receive services. The number of new slots was also based on the actual number of slots created, but it was scaled according to the larger, projected enrollment of the original plan.

This model enables us to determine the extent to which the difference between planned and actual costs can be explained by the difference between the planned and actual service mix. Because only operating and capital costs are dependent on the service mix, central administrative costs (of ECIM and UW management) remain unchanged. Total operating and capital costs were calculated in the same fashion used for the previous model, as was total cost per year and cost per child.

Table A.2

Planned Costs with Service-Mix Adjustment

Year	1996	1997	1998	1999
	0	1	2	3
Children enrolled (planned, adjusted enrollment based on actual service mix)				
Head Start–like classrooms		0	0	0
New child-care centers		0	486	1,195
Existing centers		0	68	562
New FCC homes		209	204	215
Existing homes		0	0	0
Literacy/readiness programs		0	0	0
Total		209	758	1,972
Child capacity added each year, based on actual service mix and planned enrollment				
Classrooms		0	181	0
Centers		0	582	1,658
FCC homes		498	110	355
Operating cost per child[a]				
Head Start–like classrooms		3,900	4,000	4,120
New child-care centers		7,280	7,500	7,725
Existing centers		5,720	5,890	6,060
New FCC homes		5,400	5,560	5,725
Existing homes		3,800	3,900	4,015
Literacy/readiness programs		1,000	1,000	1,000
Capital cost per child capacity (planned)				
Classrooms		759	759	759
Centers		5,000	5,000	5,000
FCC homes		200	200	200
Capital costs				
Classrooms		0	137,572	0
Centers		0	2,912,397	8,291,069
FCC homes		99,642	22,015	71,066
Total		99,642	3,071,984	8,362,135
Amortized capital costs[b]		10,940	348,227	1,266,345

Table A.2 (continued)

Year	1996	1997	1998	1999
	0	1	2	3
Operating costs				
Head Start–like classrooms		0	0	0
New child-care centers		0	3,640,955	9,234,886
Existing centers		0	401,314	3,404,894
New FCC homes		1,125,900	1,136,489	1,231,916
Existing homes		0	0	0
Literacy/readiness programs		0	0	0
Total operating costs		1,125,900	5,178,758	13,871,696
Central administrative costs	133,125	518,991	551,540	563,775
Total	133,125	1,744,533	8,802,282	22,797,606
Total with amortization	133,125	1,655,831	6,078,526	15,701,816
Cost per child-year, with amortization				
Children-years served		209	758	1,972
Capital		52	459	642
Capital as % of total		0.66	5.73	8.06
Administrative		2,489	728	286
Administrative as % of total		31.34	9.07	3.59
Operating		5,400	6,832	7,033
Operating as % of total		68.00	85.20	88.34
Total		7,942	8,019	7,961

[a]Includes inflation, which is 3 percent per year, but then rounded off.

[b]Capital costs are amortized over a 15-year period at a 7 percent interest rate.

It should be noted that in actuality, ECI created a few classrooms, but, contrary to the expectations of the original planners, the children in these programs ended up receiving full-day care. Hence, for these programs, we used the cost per child capacity assumed for classrooms ($759) to calculate capital costs, and the operating cost per child assumed for full-day centers ($7,725 for year three) to calculate operating costs.

The cost-per-child figures indicate that simply by changing the service mix of the original plan to reflect the complete use of full-day, capital-intensive programs (primarily new centers), the total cost per child-year would have been expected to increase to $7,961.

PLANNED COSTS WITH VARIABLE OPERATING COST ASSUMPTION CORRECTED

We simulated what the cost per child calculated in Table A.2 (planned costs adjusted to account for the actual service mix) might look like if the original planners had recognized that each center's operating costs would be largely fixed rather than variable. We made no adjustment for family child-care homes, where compensation was paid per child and for which operating costs are in fact variable. We used the available data on enrollment and licensed capacity in ECI programs for 1999 to estimate ECI's average enrollment level in centers as a proportion of total capacity, accounting for the fact that programs would likely build their enrollments gradually over the year.

This process involved two steps. First, we estimated the enrollment rate in ECI centers in 1999. We began by adjusting reported estimates of licensed capacity downward to reflect the fact that "ECI capacity" in each center was less than licensed capacity (because of ECI's tighter staff-to-child ratio and group size requirements); this adjustment involved multiplying licensed capacity by 88.29 percent.[2] Because we had enrollment and capacity data for only six of the 12 months of 1999, we used a linear interpolation approach to estimate values for the other six months (see Table A.3). With enrollment and capacity figures for all twelve months, we then calculated monthly average enrollment and capacity estimates. Based on these estimates, we calculated that ECI centers averaged enrollment at 72.6 percent of total ECI capacity for the year.

Second, we applied this estimate to the cost-per-child estimate presented in Table A.2. Specifically, we inflated the estimated operating cost per child in centers by dividing it by 0.726 (leaving capital and administrative costs unchanged). This adjustment may be slightly overstated, because a small part of a center's operating costs may in

---

[2]ECI records reported licensed capacity in each center. Regrettably, however, we had an accurate estimate of the lower "ECI capacity" in only one center. Lacking better information, we used the ratio of ECI capacity to licensed capacity in that center (88.29 percent) to estimate the ECI capacity of all centers. Because ECI's requirements about ratios, group sizes, and physical space were consistent across centers, we believe that this should provide a relatively accurate estimate of ECI capacity.

Table A.3

Enrollment and Capacity in ECI Centers, 1999

	Enrollment	ECI Capacity
January[a]	116	266
February[a]	160	306
March[a]	203	346
April[a]	246	387
May	317	457
June	317	457
July	354	457
August[a]	419	549
September	468	627
October[a]	506	630
November	547	663
December	600	711
Total	4,254	5,856
Enrollment/capacity		0.72645

[a]Month for which we lack data. The values for this month were estimated using ordinary least squares linear regression.

fact be variable rather than fixed. For example, centers that are less than fully enrolled will use fewer disposable supplies (e.g., crayons and books) than will fully enrolled centers. We believe these variable costs are likely to be relatively small. Our adjustment factor assumed that all costs are fixed and therefore generated an upper-bound estimate of the cost per child. (From a business planning perspective, such an adjustment might be considered prudently conservative.)

The results of this adjustment are presented in Table A.4. As shown in the table, the operating cost per child increases from $7,033 to $9,445, raising the total estimated cost per child from $7,961 to as much as $10,373. Hence, if the planners had correctly projected the service mix *and* had recognized that operating costs would be largely fixed, their expected cost per child would have been as high as $10,373. Accounting for these two mistaken assumptions explains as much as 65 percent of the difference between the planned ($4,407) and actual ($13,612) cost per child.

Table A.4

Planned Costs with Service-Mix and Fixed-Cost Adjustments

	Planned	Planned, with Actual Service Mix	Planned, with Service-Mix and Fixed-Cost Adjustments
Operating	3,966	7,033	9,445[a]
Administrative	286	286	286
Capital	155	642	642
Total	4,407	7,961	10,373

[a]Derived by inflating the operating cost in the "planned, with actual service mix" scenario using the 72.6 percent adjustment factor.

ACTUAL ECI COSTS

Finally, Table A.5 presents the actual costs of ECI in a parallel format. This analysis was limited by the availability of cost data collected by UW and ECIM. UW and former ECI staff were unable to provide us with data on total costs beyond 1999 (year three).[3] Nevertheless, 1999 was in fact the last full year of the initiative. In July 2000, the initiative was scaled down to two communities, with the remaining communities receiving a reduced amount of funding from alternative UW sources. While we were able to collect data on operating and capital costs for each type of service for 1997 and 1998, the data available for 1999 could not be disaggregated by service type.

In contrast to the previous models, total operating (capital) costs were not calculated on the basis of cost per child enrolled (per slot created) for each service type. Rather, former ECI staff collected and provided us with data on total operating, capital, and administrative costs. They also gathered and provided us with data on the number of children enrolled. We relied on their estimates of the number of

---

[3]For 1996 through 1999, the data are estimates of the full cost of ECI, including in-kind contributions given directly to ECI programs (without passing through UW). However, we believe that some in-kind contributions (such as the donation of space to a few providers by third parties) are not counted here. Thus, the actual full cost of ECI each year was probably slightly higher than our estimates suggest.

Table A.5

Actual ECI Costs

Year	1996	1997	1998	1999
	0	1	2	3
Children enrolled				
New child-care centers/classrooms		0	108	446
Existing centers		0	88	154
New FCC homes		10	37	59
Existing homes		0	0	0
Literacy/readiness programs		0	0	0
Total		10	233	659
Children enrolled, adjusted for number of months served				
New child-care centers/classrooms		0	57	300
Existing centers		0	8	141
New FCC homes		5	24	54
Existing homes		0	0	0
Literacy/readiness programs		0	0	0
Total		5	89	495
Operating costs				
New child-care centers/classrooms		0	1,229,554	NA
Existing centers		0	202,003	NA
New FCC homes		62,467	487,015	NA
Existing homes		0	0	NA
Literacy/readiness programs		0	0	NA
Total		62,467	1,918,572	5,783,390
Capital costs				
New child-care centers/classrooms		0	1,259,081	NA
Existing centers		0	66,474	NA
FCC homes		17,175	97,586	NA
Literacy/readiness programs		0	0	NA
Total		17,175	1,423,141	1,703,056
Capital costs, amortized[a]				
New child-care centers/classrooms		0	138,240	NA
Existing centers		0	7,298	NA
FCC homes		1,886	10,714	NA
Literacy/readiness programs		0	0	NA
Total		1,886	158,139	345,125

Table A.5 (continued)

Year	1996	1997	1998	1999
	0	1	2	3
Central administrative costs	365,344	634,079	754,372	609,538
Total	365,344	713,721	4,096,085	8,095,985
Total with amortization	365,344	698,432	2,831,083	6,738,054
Cost per child-year, with amortization				
Children-years served		5	89	495
Operating		12,493	21,518	11,684
Capital		377	1,774	697
Administrative		126,816	8,461	1,231
Total		139,686	31,753	13,612
Administrative as % of total				9.05
Capital as % of total				5.12
Operating as % of total				85.83
Cost per child-hour, with amortization				
Child-hours[b]		13,000	231,400	1,287,000
Operating		4.81	8.29	4.49
Capital		0.15	0.68	0.27
Administrative		48.78	3.26	0.47
Total		53.73	12.23	5.24

[a]Capital costs are amortized over a 15-year period at a 7 percent interest rate.

[b]Assumes that 12 months served equals 260 service days per child, and that all care provided was full-day care, at an average of 10 hours per child per day.

NOTE: NA = data not available.

months per year that each child received services, which we used to adjust the total enrollment figures to accurately reflect the amount of services actually provided. ECIM did not closely track the amount of time each child received services. Thus, the ECIM estimates are based on the number of children receiving services at the end of the year and the opening dates of each program. This method is likely to produce generous adjusted enrollment estimates. In particular, it is likely to underestimate the amount of time that programs needed to build their enrollments, therefore overstating enrollment to some extent. Nevertheless, lacking better data, we relied on these estimates. Even with this generous method for adjusting enrollment numbers, the estimated cost per child is $13,612, which is substantially higher than expected.

This cost-per-child estimate was calculated in the same way it was calculated in the previous models. The total cost is the sum of total operating, capital, and central administrative costs. The total cost (amortized) was then divided by the total adjusted number of children enrolled to produce the cost per child per year.

Cost per child-hour was also calculated as before. Reflecting reports from lead agencies and providers that virtually all children were in full-day service, we assumed that 100 percent of the children enrolled received 10 hours of care per day. To the extent that any children received part-day care, the resulting cost per child-hour ($5.24 in 1999) understates the true cost. This cost per child-hour can be compared to the cost per child-hour estimated by our model of the original plan ($3.02). The comparison suggests that even when adjusting for the intensity of the services provided (as measured by hours in care), the difference between expected and actual costs remains substantial, a finding consistent with our results based on the cost per child-year.

REFERENCES

Anderson, Patricia M., and Phillip B. Levine (1999, Mar). *Child Care and Mothers' Employment Decisions.* Cambridge, MA: National Bureau of Economic Research, Working Paper 7058.

The Annie E. Casey Foundation (1995). *The Path of Most Resistance: Reflections on Lessons Learned from New Futures.* Baltimore, MD: The Annie E. Casey Foundation.

Bagnato, S.J. (2002). *Quality Early Learning—Key to School Success: A First-Phase Program Evaluation Research Report for Pittsburgh's Early Childhood Initiative (ECI).* Pittsburgh, PA: Children's Hospital of Pittsburgh, SPECS Evaluation Research Team.

Barnett, S.W. (1995). "Long-Term Effects of Early Childhood Programs on Cognitive and School Outcomes," *The Future of Children,* 5:25–50.

Besharov, Douglas J. (ed.) (1996). *Enhancing Early Childhood Programs: Burdens and Opportunities.* Washington, D.C.: Child Welfare League of America Press and American Enterprise Institute.

Blau, David M. (2001). *The Child Care Problem: An Economic Analysis.* New York: Russell Sage.

Brown-Lyons, Melanie, Anne Robertson, and Jean Layzer (2001). *Kith and Kin—Informal Care: Highlights from Recent Research.* New York: National Center for Children in Poverty, Mailman School of Public Health, Columbia University.

Campbell, Frances A., Elizabeth Pungello, Shari Miller-Johnson, Margaret Burchinal, and Craig T. Ramey (2001). "The Development of Cognitive and Academic Abilities: Growth Curves from an Early Childhood Educational Experiment," *Developmental Psychology*, 37:231–242.

Campbell, Frances A., Craig T. Ramey, Elizabeth Pungello, Joseph Sparling, and Shari Miller-Johnson (2002). "Early Childhood Education: Young Adult Outcomes from the Abecedarian Project," *Applied Developmental Science*, 6(1):42–57.

Carnegie Corporation of New York (1994). *Starting Points: Meeting the Needs of Our Youngest Children.*

Center for the Study of Social Policy (1995, May). *Building New Futures for At-Risk Youth: Findings from a Five Year, Multi-Site Evaluation.* Washington, D.C.: CSSP.

Center for the Study of Social Policy (1996, Sep). *Systems Change at the Neighborhood Level: Creating Better Futures for Children, Youth, and Families.* Washington, D.C.: CSSP.

Committee on Ways and Means (2000, Oct 6). *2000 Green Book, Overview of Entitlement Programs.* Washington, D.C.: United States House of Representatives.

Cryer, Debby, and Margaret Burchinal (1995, Jun). "Parents as Child Care Consumers," in Suzanne W. Helburn (ed.), *Cost, Quality, and Child Outcomes in Child Care Centers: Technical Report.* Denver, CO: Department of Economics, Center for Research in Economic and Social Policy, University of Colorado.

Dickerson & Mangus, Ink. (1999, Sep 7). *The Early Childhood Initiative: External Stakeholder Research and Recommendations.* Pittsburgh, PA: Dickerson & Mangus, Ink.

Education Week (2002, Jan 10). *Quality Counts 2002: Building Blocks for Success.* Annual Report of *Education Week.* http://www.edweek.org/sreports/qc02/index.html.

Ehrle, Jennifer, Gina Adams, and Kathryn Tout (2001, Jan). *Who's Caring for Our Youngest Children? Child Care Patterns of Infants and Toddlers.* New York: The Urban Institute.

Farber, Anne E., Jeanne E. Williams, and Christina J. Groark (1994, Jun). *Overcoming the Odds: Another Look: Children Facing Uncertain Futures in Pittsburgh and Allegheny County*. Pittsburgh, PA: University of Pittsburgh Office of Child Development.

Fuller, Bruce, and Sharon Lynn Kagan (2000, Feb). *Remember the Children: Mothers Balance Work and Child Care Under Welfare Reform*. Berkeley, CA: Graduate School of Education-PACE, University of California.

Gormley, William T. (1995). *Everybody's Children*. Washington, D.C.: Brookings Institution.

Guralnick, M.J. (ed.) (1997). *Effectiveness of Early Intervention*. Baltimore, MD: Paul Brookes Publishing

Helburn, Suzanne W. (ed.) (1995). *Cost, Quality, and Outcomes in Child Care Centers: Technical Report*. Denver, CO: Department of Economics, Center for Research in Economic and Social Policy, University of Colorado.

Helburn, Suzanne W., and Barbara R. Bergmann (2002). *America's Child Care Problem: The Way Out*. New York: Palgrave.

Hofferth, Sandra L., Kimberlee A. Shauman, Robin R. Henke, and Jerry West (1998, Jun). *Characteristics of Children's Early Care and Education Programs: Data from the 1995 National Household Education Survey*. Washington, D.C.: U.S. Department of Education, National Center for Education Statistics, NCES 98–128.

Howes, Carollee (1997). "Children's Experiences in Center Based Child Care as a Function of Teacher Background and Adult:Child Ratio," *Merrill-Palmer Quarterly*, 43(3):404–425.

Howes, Carollee, Ellen Galinsky, Marybeth Shinn, Leyla Gulcur, Margaret Clements, Annette Sibley, Martha Abbott-Shim, and Jan McCarthy (1998). *The Florida Child Care Quality Improvement Study: 1996 Report*. New York: Families and Work Institute.

Karoly, Lynn A., Peter W. Greenwood, Susan S. Everingham, Jill Houbé, M. Rebecca Kilburn, C. Peter Rydell, Matthew Sanders, and James R. Chiesa (1998). *Investing in Our Children: What We*

Know and Don't Know About the Costs and Benefits of Early Childhood Interventions. Santa Monica, CA: RAND. MR-898.

Karoly, Lynn A., M. Rebecca Kilburn, J.H. Bigelow, Jonathan P. Caulkins, and Jill Cannon (2001). *Assessing Costs and Benefits of Early Childhood Intervention Programs: Overview and Application to the Starting Early Starting Smart Program.* Santa Monica, CA: RAND. MR-1336.

National Center for Children in Poverty (2001, Oct). *Learning from Starting Points: Findings from the Starting Points Assessment Project.* New York: Columbia University.

National Center for Children in Poverty (2000). *Map and Track: State Initiatives for Young Children and Families.* New York: Columbia University.

National Research Council (2001). *Getting to Positive Outcomes for Children in Child Care: A Summary of Two Workshops.* Washington, D.C.: National Academy Press.

NICHD Early Child Care Research Network (1999). "Child Outcomes When Child Care Centers Meet Recommended Standards for Quality," *American Journal of Public Health*, 89:1072–1077.

NICHD Early Child Care Research Network (2000). "The Relation of Child Care to Cognitive and Language Development," *Child Development*, 71:960–980.

Peisner-Feinberg, Ellen S., and Margaret R. Burchinal (1997). "Relations Between Pre-School Children's Child-Care Experiences and Concurrent Development: The Cost, Quality, and Outcomes Study," *Merrill-Palmer Quarterly*, 43:451–477.

Peisner-Feinberg, Ellen S., Margaret R. Burchinal, Richard M. Clifford, Noreen Yazejian, Mary L. Culkin, Janice Zelazo, Carollee Howes, Patricia Byler, Sharon Lynn Kagan, and Jean Rustici (1999). *The Children of the Cost, Quality, and Outcomes Study Go to School.* Chapel Hill, NC: Frank Porter Graham Child Development Center, University of North Carolina.

Reynolds, Arthur J. (2000). *Success in Early Intervention: The Chicago Child-Parent Centers.* Lincoln, NE: University of Nebraska Press.

Reynolds, Arthur J., Judy A. Temple, Dylan L. Robertson, and Emily A Mann (2001). "Long-Term Effects of an Early Childhood Intervention on Educational Achievement and Juvenile Arrest: A 15-Year Follow-up of Low-Income Children in Public Schools," *Journal of the American Medical Association*, 285:2339–2346

Ruopp, Richard, Jeffrey Travers, Frederic Glantz, and Craig Coelen (1979). *Children at the Center*. Cambridge, MA: Abt Books.

Schorr, Lisbeth B. (with Daniel Schorr) (1989). *Within Our Reach. Breaking the Cycle of Disadvantage*. New York: Doubleday.

Schorr, Lisbeth B. (1997). *Common Purpose: Strengthening Families and Neighborhoods to Rebuild America*. New York: Doubleday.

Schweinhart, Lawrence J., Helen V. Barnes, and David P. Weikart (1993). *Significant Benefits: The High/Scope Perry Preschool Study Through Age 27*. Ypsilanti, MI: High/Scope Educational Research Foundation.

Smith, Kristin (2000). *Who's Minding the Kids? Child Care Arrangements: Fall 1995*. Washington, D.C.: U.S. Census Bureau. Current Population Reports, P70-70.

Sonenstein, Freya L. (1991). "The Child Care Preferences of Parents with Young Children," in Janet S. Hyde and Marilyn J. Essex (eds.), *Parental Leave and Child Care: A Research and Policy Agenda*. Philadelphia, PA: Temple University Press.

U.S. General Accounting Office (1997). *Head Start Research Provides Little Information on Impact of Current Program*. Washington, D.C.: GAO.

Vandell, Debra Lowe, and Barbara Wolfe (2000). *Child Care Quality: Does It Matter and Does It Need to Be Improved?* Madison, WI: Institute for Research on Poverty, University of Wisconsin-Madison.

Walker, James (1991). "Public Policy and the Supply of Child Care Services," in David Blau (ed.), *The Economics of Child Care*. New York: Russell Sage Foundation.

Walsh, Joan (1998). "The Eye of the Storm: Ten Years on the Front Lines of New Futures. An Interview with Otis Johnson and Don Crary." Baltimore, MD: The Annie E. Casey Foundation.

Yoshikawa, H. (1995, Winter). "Long-Term Effects of Early Childhood Programs on Social Outcomes and Delinquency," *The Future of Children*, 5:51–75.

Zigler, Edward, and Susan Muenchow (1992). *Head Start: The Inside Story of America's Most Successful Educational Experiment*. New York: Basic Books.

Zigler, Edward, Sharon Lynn Kagan, and Nancy W. Hall (eds.) (1996). *Children, Families, and Government: Preparing for the Twenty-First Century*. New York: Cambridge University Press.